DAVID EDMONDSON

THE PRODIGAL FATHER

"But when he was a great way off, his father saw him…"

Published by

CHRISTIAN DAY
Publishing   Co.   ™
6148 Jones Road, Flowery Branch, GA 30542

Contents

Acknowledgements

My Mom: You have always done the best you could in every situation. All the times Daddy didn't show up, you were there to piece me back together. You took the brunt of a lot of my anger and pain. I love you and I am glad you are my Mom.

Jerry Leaphart: You are my son and I love you with every part of me. My family is blessed to have you in it. My staff is better because you are a part. Our church is the greatest because you help lead us to Him. You are forever "The Bomb"!

Lynn and Mike Queen: Lynn, you are more than an assistant; you are so often my stability. You are CCChurch's MawMaw, our Queen, and our Obededom. Mike, you are an amazing man. Your passion and compassion are inspiring. You are CCChurch's PawPaw, our Queenie, and our Road Captain.

Pat McWhorter: You tirelessly train and disciple men to carry the Gospel into all the world. You and your family have supported me for many years. Your love for God and desire for His truth and wisdom is second to none. The work you have put into this book, as well as all the other literature you have been a part of, will echo throughout all eternity.

My Staff: I would like to thank you all for your dedication to Stephanie and me. You ladies and gentlemen are the definition of hard work, passion, faithfulness, and compassion. I love you with all my heart!

CCChurch: Stephanie and I love you all so much! You all are Revival Carriers! Keep loving Jesus; keep seeking His glory and keep chasing Him! Together has Power! Together we win! Heart and Soul.

Dedication

I dedicate this book to my spiritual parents, Pastor Todd and Pastor Karen Smith. Stephanie and I have always fought for you, loved you, stood by you, dreamed with you and we have never stopped!

When no one believed in us, you guys did. Your wisdom and direction have always been a safe place for us to draw from. Your passion to love Jesus inspires us to do the same. Your love for His people motivates us to love them, too. Your heart for revival has been imparted to us and, for that, we are forever thankful!

Pastor Todd, you have brought so much healing to my heart over the years. You have been more of a father to me than anyone in my life. My dad never took me fishing. He never took me to travel the world. He never took me to play golf. He never took me hunting. He never helped me with my marriage. He never showed me how to be a husband. He never helped me be a better dad. He never taught me business. He never taught me how to handle people. He never prepared a future for me and my family. He never gave me an opportunity to succeed. He never believed in me. And he never taught me what it means to love Jesus and live for him.

You have done all these things and so much more. You are a good man, Pastor! You are my Prodigal Father and I want to say, Thank you, with all my heart!

Pastor Karen, you are THE MOST passionate person I have ever met. You love hard. You love Jesus hard. You love your husband, your boys, and your family hard. You love me and my family hard, as well.

Your love for God is inspiring, your wisdom is intimidating, your anointing is superior to most, and the authority from which you speak is fierce! You are God's General!

I love you both!

Summary

I will begin this journey by using an introduction that was used to introduce me to the platform of a speaking engagement some years ago.

A dear friend of mine was leading a church in the hills of Virginia and I would often speak for him and his congregation. He and I held conferences around the southern US, as well in other countries. We grew up in ministry together and knew each other pretty well.

I was asked to minister at his Bible College on a special evening. I will never forget when he took the microphone to introduce me, with a large grin on his face, trying to mask the serious concern he had. He made this introduction: "I would like to bring to the platform now one of my best friends. He and I have been friends for a long time and I love him and his family very much. But I want to say, I will not be held responsible for anything he says!"

So I want to begin this book with the same kind of warning.

What you are about to read is not meant to just enlighten you on a subject, or for your pleasure and enjoyment alone. I am writing this book with one major desire in my mind and heart. That desire and hope is to show you that no matter what kind of father you have or had in life, there is a Father who is GOOD!

He is loving, faithful, generous, kind, and full of passion for His children.

If you are looking for literature that is safe to read, this book is NOT for you! If your desire is to enjoy a fictional book, full of funny stories and motivating accounts of one's life, this book is NOT for you!

I am not writing to give you sermon topics, principles or patterns for successful living, revelatory inspiration, or theological building blocks for your religious life structure.

I am writing this book to rescue the forsaken. To extend a hand of hope to one who may be drowning in a sea of rejection.

My prayer is that, by the end of this book, you will be able to see Jesus as your Father, and that your view of Him will clearly reveal who He really is, rather than seeing Him through the failures of your earthly father.

I will NOT hold back! Some of the details I will speak of in the following pages will probably make you uncomfortable. Some of the verbiage that I will use to paint the picture of my reality will not be very restricted. You will be reading my reality. You will be given details into just some of the events in my life that made me the man I am today, but also incarcerated my true identity and made it hard for me to love and trust a God who refers to Himself as my Father.
You will not read of fictional characters. You will not be examining imagined events. What you will be exposed to is one boy's/one young man's/one adult man's experiences with his natural dad.

Some of the events will be shocking. Some of the details may make you want to stop reading, close the book, and throw it on a shelf. However, I assure you that if you will keep reading and allow Holy Spirit to minister to your own personal pain that will surface, this book will possibly be the most healing book you have ever read.

Our heavenly Father has been stuck behind walls we have built because our relationships with our natural fathers were not good.

Through the pages of this book, God will show Himself to you. He will reveal His true character. You will realize God is not the Father that you are trying to protect yourself from. He is NOT the daddy that left you! He is not the stepdad that mistreated you! He is LOVE. He will hold you, love you, protect you, and provide for you!

Take this journey with me as I introduce you to the reality of who God is. Join me as I reveal to you The Prodigal Father.

Chapter 1

My First Memories…

Life on the Hooch

My earliest memories come from the front yard of my MawMaw's trailer.

Yes I said MawMaw and trailer.

The old home place of the Edmondson family was located on the banks of the Chattahoochee River in a small town in North Georgia called Duluth. Though it has grown dramatically over the last thirty-five years, Duluth had only one gas station and one fruit stand when I was a boy.

No grocery stores, no shopping malls, no Starbucks, and no theaters.

The only gas station was owned by my uncle Whitey. It was named Whitey and Eddie's Duluth One Stop. It was a landmark in the community for decades, marked by a huge iron statue of Uncle Whitey standing at the front entrance with a huge cigar in his mouth.

You would never see Uncle Whitey without that cigar. As a kid, I was filled with pride when my buddies and I would ride our bikes to the Duluth One Stop and Uncle Whitey would give me a free Icee.

Uncle Whitey was larger than life. He was more popular than the governor, and had a heart so big that he never let anyone go without. From giving away food, paying for the local high school's football uniforms, and secretly paying off others' debts, to just bringing stability to a town that was just establishing its identity, Uncle Whitey did whatever he could to help those around him.

Across the street stood Ted's Fruit stand. It was a small white block building with fruits and vegetables sitting on and hanging from every inch of the place. It was owned by one of my daddy's best friends, Ted Hammrick.

Ted was a great guy like Uncle Whitey. He would give me an apple or an orange, sometimes a bag of boiled peanuts or a handful of fresh grapes. Along with the treat, Ted would always give me a big hug and say, "How are you doing, Little David?" (I was named after my daddy, John David Edmondson, Sr. So, everyone around Duluth and in my family called me Little David.)

I didn't mind the nickname. As a matter of fact I was proud to be called Little David. My daddy was my hero. I would bend my ball cap like he bent his. I would go without a shirt, wear cut off jean shorts, stick my belly out, and even say a random curse word from time to time when adults were not around. All because I wanted to be just like my daddy.

I didn't get to see my daddy very often, but every chance I could, I would jump on my bike and trek across town to Ted's Fruit Stand or The Duluth One Stop in search of one moment with my superman.

Often times, I would ride up and Uncle Whitey would be standing outside the store talking to customers. He would always greet me with a huge hug and call me "Little David!"

I would always ask him if he had seen Daddy or if he knew where he was. Many times his answer was, "No, I haven't seen him in a few days," or "Well, Little David, your daddy is in jail."

Most of the time, my excitement to feel Daddy's embrace was met with that kind of letdown. I would jump back on my bike and cross the two-lane street to Ted's Fruit Stand in hopes that maybe Daddy was there shelling peanuts and drinking a cold Budweiser.

Usually, however, the response was the same. Daddy was just not there or he was in jail.

My sister, cousins, and I rode many miles on those old bicycles, jumping makeshift ramps in the woods, riding without grasping the hand grips of the handle bars. Sometimes one hand would grip the handlebar, while the other was grasping an Icee from Uncle Whitey's store or an ice-cream we had purchased at Dairy Queen.

We grew up in a time when it was safe for kids to take off at daylight and not come home until dark. We watched out for each other. At any given time, we might have caught the woods on fire, swiped a Fireball jawbreaker from the local butchery, or got a black eye fighting the neighbors' kids, but all things considered, we were just good kids growing up in a small country town.

We had no cell phones, no gaming stations, no vapes (although we may or may not have swiped a Marlboro Red or two in our time), and we had no means of travel except our feet or our bikes. We learned to live by our own experiences. We resolved conflict by working it out or fighting it out amongst ourselves.

The key was we took care of it ourselves. We didn't run home to Mommy or Daddy, because often enough, there was not a mommy or daddy to run home to.

My daddy's side of the family lived on the banks of a river. To get to the property, you had to go past a fish hatchery, follow a long gravel driveway, and cross a small bridge over the river. Then you arrived!

My childhood paradise was a few acres of green grass bordered by the river on one side and a huge hay field on the other. On one end of the property stood my grandfather's building where he made and sold chicken coops, and on the other end was my grandparents' single-wide mobile home. Back in the day, we only knew them as trailers. It wasn't much, but to me it was heaven.

It was in that beautiful green grass that I learned to drive.

Yep, as a very young child, I would jump in my grandmother's lap and off we would go, making circle after circle around the yard. I would steer and MawMaw would control the gas and brake pedals.

It was also in this grassy paradise that I would receive my first gift from my daddy. It was a go-cart with a five horsepower engine and no brakes. That's right - no brakes. My daddy would stand on the back of the go-cart and when we needed to slow down or stop, he would yell, "Take your foot off the gas!" And he would slam his feet on the ground and bring the cart to a very long stop. This was when I experienced my first accident.

My sister was driving the go-cart and Daddy was perched on the back like an umpire intently gazing over the back of a catcher on the baseball field. They came flying around the backside of the trailer when I had the bright idea of turning a cartwheel in front of them just as they flew by. I mean, surely a cartwheel would bring the drama and excitement we needed to cap off the fastest lap in the history of go-carting!

Well my timing was off, and just as my head was towards the ground and my feet in the air, the go-cart ran me over. A go-cart with a five-year-old girl driving and a twenty-year-old man hanging on the back, colliding with a four-year-old boy! That was no match at all!

The collision busted my head open, and a hospital visit was next on the list of events for the day.

If that wasn't bad enough, my dad, the brake man, jumped off the go-cart to swoop me up and care for me. He failed to realize my sister was still on the cart, barreling straight towards the river! To make a long story short, my stepmother ran down the go-cart and saved my sister from using the go-cart as a diving board straight into the Chattahoochee River!

Life on the Hooch was great for the most part. It was here that I learned to drive. I learned the value of family time. I learned to wade on the slippery rocks of a rushing river. It was at this old home place that I learned so many life lessons that would shape me into the man I was becoming.

But not all the lessons were good ones.

I had a cousin that I thought was *The Man*! He was six years older than me, and therefore, someone who really impacted my early years. He could climb trees I couldn't even reach. He could reach the gas and brake pedals in MawMaw's car. He could outrun the wind and climb a stack of chicken coops faster than anyone. He could also steal cold beer from Daddy's cooler without anyone knowing.

5

Daddy used to tell us to go and grab him a beer out of the cooler. I mean this is the main reason you have children, right? To fetch you a cold beverage while you relax by the river, resting in the rays of the setting sun, and smacking "skeeters" as they bite and suck the blood from your arms.

Well, this is where I learned I could not keep up with my daddy drinking cold beer. Every time I would grab Daddy a beer, my cousin would pocket one and I would snag a drink of Daddy's on the way to deliver it. I just wanted to be like my dad!

He made drinking beer look so fun! Sweating to death in the hot, Georgia sun, after running laps around the trailer, turning cartwheels and daring to make a quick climb up and back down the twelve-foot stack of chicken coops, of course a young boy needs to refuel with a cold beverage!

So that's what my cousin and I did.

Not realizing our equilibrium was being highly affected by the continual refueling, we thought we were being so sly! We had no idea until later in life that Daddy had drunk enough beers to know when his beer had been tampered with. But he never said a word. He would just smile as we ran off sideways into the grass.

You may be asking yourself, Why is he sharing these events with me? What does any of this have to do with me realizing who God is as my Father?

Well these first memories are very important to the establishment of the role of my earthly father in my life.

For instance, I had a natural longing for my daddy. I would chase him around town just for the possibility of a few seconds in his strong embrace or a few affirming words.

I saw at a very early age that spending time with me was not high on my daddy's list of priorities.

In spite of all his failures, my daddy was still my standard of manhood.

These were some of my earliest memories as a child: running after my father, and searching for or reaching out for a father who, most often, was not reaching back.

Other relationships I had in my life inevitably were influenced by the absence of my Father or the bone-headed decisions he was making while battling his own addictions.

My concept of father-son relationships was being formed with every turn of a bicycle wheel, much like a vessel on a pottery wheel. As I rode looking for, longing for, that time with Daddy, my view of his acceptance and what pleased him was being ingrained in me on the banks of the river.

It was okay to ride go-carts with no brakes. It was okay to steal cold beer from Daddy's cooler at four and five years of age, and drink them. Daddy would laugh when I yelled a curse word at a mosquito bite. I heard him do the same. His laughter was the validation I was longing for.

Life on the Hooch. It was so much fun! But later I would see it as the genesis of my unstable foundations.

The Trip to Talladega Speedway

One of the best known races in the NASCAR Racing Circuit is run at Talladega Motor Speedway.

It is hugely popular because of the high speeds the drivers can push their cars to. As NASCAR's longest oval track, it is 2.66 miles long, allowing drivers to reach speeds of over 200 mile per hour. It's loud, it's crazy, it's dangerous, and it is fun!

Tickets for Talladega Motor Speedway are some of the hardest to purchase for any sport. One weekend a year, 175,000 crazed and mostly drunk racing fans act out some of their worst behaviors together and, well, get stupid!

It is a redneck tradition and, according to my daddy, a great place to take your five-year-old son.

My daddy pulled into the driveway of the duplex where my mother and her new husband lived. My cousins and I were around back hitting bumblebees with an oversized, red plastic baseball bat. Just one of the many hobbies we had!

Other hobbies included catching lightning bugs at night and putting them in Mason jars, catching flying beetles and tying a string to their legs, flying them around like kites. We also played Spotlight, which is a very *safe* game to encourage your children to play. A bunch of kids get together once it's very dark outside. One kid takes a flashlight while the rest run wildly in the dark to find a place to hide. Then the flashlight kid goes to find them, shining the light on fleeing kids and shouting, "Spotlight on Jason!" Or "Spotlight on Christy!" He had to get the person's name right that he was spotlighting, and he had to run around the yard in the dark while avoiding trees, bushes, holes in the ground, and, the dozen other kids running frantically in the dark!

Dangerous? You might say so!

Anyway, Daddy pulled into the driveway and, once I knew
he was there, I dropped everything and ran to see him. I had
no idea he was coming. I had no idea I was going to spend
the weekend with him, but once I found out, I was ecstatic! I
don't think my Mom wanted to tell me Daddy was coming to
get me, in case he didn't show up – which is what happened
most of the time.

I jumped in the truck and perched in the middle of the bench
seat of my daddy's friend's truck. Actually, I was mostly
standing and jumping to the country music blaring through
the speakers. Seat belt usage was not mandatory at that time
in Georgia, so, for me to be standing on the bench seat of a
truck really was not abnormal. Most of the time, in cars, you
would find us fighting over who got to lie on top of the back
seats between the backrests and the rear window. I slept
many hours under the rear window of a car.

I don't remember a lot about the ride to the speedway, but I
could never forget seeing all those people and cars and
campers as we pulled into the pit area. It was unbelievable!
The first place Daddy took me was onto the track at one of
the corners. (In those days, security was not what it is now.) I
remember Daddy laughing at me as I tried to stay upright
while walking up the huge, banked corners of the track. It
was amazing!

It rained a lot earlier in the week and the whole infield was
nothing but mud. My daddy - being the safe, shy, intelligent
man that he was - had what I guess he thought was a great
idea. He found the hood to a wrecked car. They tied the hood
of the car to a rope, and the rope to a four-wheeler. For hours
they pulled my daddy around, behind that four-wheeler. Up
and down this huge hill in the pit area. They drug him all

9

over the infield at Talladega Motor Speedway while people cheered, laughed, and had the best time.

Monday morning on the front page of the newspaper was a picture of Daddy covered from head to toe in mud, with a big smile on his face. They called him The Mud Man and told how he entertained the crowd all evening long.

This solidified him as my hero! My daddy, the king of the show! The guy everyone wanted to be.

When Daddy got off the hood of that car, there was a line of people who couldn't wait to jump on top of that old car hood and be pulled through the mud. I was having the time of my young life. My dad was the talk of the whole infield. Everywhere we went, people waved and yelled out, "Hey, Mud Man!" as they gave him a huge smile and offered him a cold beer.

The Mud Man - he was my daddy. I know it may sound stupid to you, but I was so proud he was my daddy.

Later that night - or should I say, early the next morning when we were going to sleep - Daddy pulled out a single sleeping bag. For those who may not know what a sleeping bag is, it is basically a semi-waterproof blanket that you drape over you and it zips up one side to form a warm enclosure around you. We had no camper, no vehicle, no hotel room, no bed to rest on. It was just me and my daddy zipped up in a sleeping bag laid out on the muddy ground.

I have never felt more comfortable and safe!

When the sun rose over the Talladega track the next morning, I was awakened by my dad's friend's panicked voice exclaiming, "Where is Little David?"

I will never forget my daddy smiling and pointing down into the sleeping bag and saying, "He is right here." I had curled up way down in the sleeping bag to keep warm and safe. It was in this moment that I realized, my daddy was my protector. He was not going to let anything happen to me! I didn't need a fancy five-star hotel room. I didn't need a million-dollar Prevost camper. I didn't even need a security guard to stand his post while I slept.

All I needed was to curl up at the feet of my daddy inside an old sleeping bag and trust that he would not let anything bad happen to me.

It was the day of the big race. As my dad and his friends were watching the race, my assignment was to walk around the infield and pick up empty beer and soda cans and throw them in the back of the truck. Every time I would bring in an arm full of cans Daddy would smile at me and say, "Good job, Buddy. Go get some more."

I thought I was on some kind of scavenger hunt adventure. I didn't know at the time that Daddy was going to take all the cans to the local recycling place and get money for them. But I didn't care. I picked up cans for hours that day in the blistering sun. With my cut-off blue jean shorts, my bent-up baseball cap, and no shirt, I was looking just like my daddy. Even though I was hot, tired, sleepy, hungry, and thirsty, I gathered as many cans as I could, just to be rewarded with the smile on my daddy's face and to hear him tell me I was doing a good job.

I don't remember one moment of the drive back home. I slept the whole four-hour drive. We got home and I couldn't wait to tell my Mom all about my weekend with Daddy. But things didn't go as expected. As soon as I excitingly opened the door to go inside, my Mom saw me and she went crazy!

Here was her dirty, nasty, and severely sunburned five-year-old son. My dad never thought of putting sunscreen on me. (As a matter of fact, I'm not sure there was anything such as sunscreen back then.) Either way, I was toasted, and my Mom went off.

I don't remember what was said, but one thing I do remember is what I was thinking as Mom fussed at Daddy and I noticed his smile quickly turn to disappointment. I distinctly remember thinking that I desperately didn't want Momma to make Daddy upset, because he would never take me with him again.

I wasn't thinking about the sunburn. I did think that my Mother was correct in her anger. I just didn't want Daddy to leave and not come back to take me with him again.

I remember feeling like the greatest weekend of my young life didn't end so well.

My hero, my superman, my buddy, was all of a sudden the bad guy and I was stuck in the middle. I was the reason for the conflict between Mom and Dad.

I remember Daddy leaving, and I wondered when, if ever, he would come back to get me again.

Throwing Horseshoes Under the Shade Trees

The only house my daddy ever lived in as I was growing up was nothing to write home about. It was a standard single-wide mobile home sitting on about an acre of land. The property was surrounded by a chain-linked fence and sat right on the edge of a main road. Daddy didn't own the property. He rented the home from a man whose nickname was Muscle, or, as some people called him, Hog Head.

It sounds funny, but every man in Duluth, Georgia, back then had a nickname. In the South, a nickname shows camaraderie, acceptance, love, and it identifies a person as being part of a family or group.

To this day I have nicknames for most people in my life. If you ask anyone who knows me well, they will tell you that I am awful at remembering people's names. However, I never forget someone's nickname. As strange as it seems, I think nicknames remain in my memory because of my upbringing. Every one of my daddy's friends had a nickname. For most of them, I never even knew their given names.

Hog Head or Muscle was given those names for two reasons. He was called Hog Head because he had a very large, above average sized head. I know it sounds mean but men in those days wanted a nickname to show that they were accepted in the group, and most of the nicknames were given to identify a special quality or a difference in someone. For instance he was given the nickname, Muscle, because he had no right bicep. He was born with a right bicep, but it was shot off while fighting with one of his neighbors. It wasn't long after that fight that Hog Head got his revenge. He went back to the man's house and castrated him.

I know that you must be thinking something along the lines of, "Why in the world is he writing about nicknames and gun shots?" Or "Why am I even reading this book?"

I am telling you these things to build a foundation from which I want to bring a revelation of The Father. I have to show you where I came from. What I was exposed to. To explain to you some of the events that made me who I am today. I am telling you about Hog Head so that you will understand that I was raised in violence and instability. Hog Head was my daddy's landlord, but he was also his business partner. My daddy and Hog Head sold methamphetamines together. It is from this partnership that I draw many of my childhood memories. Most of which are not very pleasant.

I can distinctly remember being placed in situations that were not safe for anyone, especially a young child. Most children have memories of visiting places like theme parks, camping venues, or sporting events. My memories, however, derive from whore houses, drug houses, chicken fights, and parties at the river bank. These are the places I went with my dad.

The funny thing is that I didn't mind going to these places. As a matter of fact, I wanted to go to these places. I wanted to go because I wanted to be with Daddy. It didn't matter to me what I saw, what kind of danger I was placed in, or what lies I had to tell when I got back home. I just longed to be with my daddy. So I would go anytime, anywhere, and experience anything, just to be around my hero.

He could trust me with his secrets. I knew it and he knew it.

Daddy knew that no matter what I saw him do, when we got home I would stick by what he told me to say. I was like a locked vault. When asked by my stepmother or mother where we had been or what was Daddy doing while we were gone all weekend, I would stick to the story. I would protect my daddy at all cost.

I needed, I longed for, his trust. I was taught to lie, cheat, and manipulate things at a very young age. I didn't realize what I was doing was wrong. I was just acting like my hero. I was longing for his love and acceptance so strongly that, no matter what it cost me, I was willing to pay the price. I would trade a thousand words of affirmation from Mom, or anyone else, for one hint of acceptance from Daddy.

The horseshoe pit was one of the first places I remember receiving this acceptance and validation. In Daddy's front yard stood two large oak trees. They were so large that they brought shade to a large portion of the yard. This was not good for the grass but it was great for us to hide under and throw horseshoes.

In Georgia, the days can get very hot and extremely humid during the spring and summer months. But these are the best days to be outside. We would sit under those two big shade trees and eat watermelon, drink cold beverages and play different games or just shoot the bull.

Shooting the bull is basically just sitting around wasting time, making up stories or lying about how big the fish were we had caught the day before.

Our favorite game to play under those two big oak trees was horseshoes. It's a simple southern yard game. You drive a metal stake in the ground on one end of the yard and another about thirty feet away. Then you take turns throwing colored, oversized horseshoes at the stakes. You accumulate points by getting closest to the stakes or throwing your horseshoe around the stake.

If you could throw your horseshoe where it would land surrounding the stake, it was called a ringer. This is what yields the most points. I can close my eyes and still hear the

15

sound of the horseshoes clanging against those metal stakes and Daddy hollering out, "That's Five!"

Five points is how many points you get with each ringer. Someone throwing a ringer would get Daddy so excited he would react by throwing his hands in the air and yelling, "That's Five!" I can still see and hear him now, throwing up his hands and yelling while spilling his Budweiser down his arm, sometimes dropping his cigarette to the ground.

Daddy loved to drink cold beer, smoke Marlboro Reds, and play horseshoes.

My love for the game was in what came before the first shoe was ever thrown. It was the time when we would choose teams. Daddy would, most all the time, if given the choice, choose me to be his partner. He would say, "I'll take Bubba."

Here comes the nickname usage again. Remember EVERYONE in those days had a nickname. I had two. A lot of people called me Little David, but those who were real close to us and family members always called me Bubba. Now in the South, Bubba is a very common nickname. Every family has at least one Bubba in the family. I was the Bubba for our family. Daddy always called me Bubba. I can never recall Daddy calling me any other name than Bubba. (Well, I can recall a few other names he would call me when the occasion warranted, names that I will not tell you because it would be un-Christian of me.)

I would hurry out to the shade trees and stand across from Daddy so I could not only hear his validation but also see him point me out of the group. No one wanted me and Daddy to play together because we usually won the game. It was like that with anything we did together. We were so competitive that we would do whatever it took to win. When

16

we would play Rook, Daddy would have signs for me to let me know what cards he had and what card he wanted me to play next. It all centered around his ashtray. If he had the Rook card he would set his cigarette in a certain slot on the ashtray. If he didn't, he would set it on a different spot. He would rub his face a certain way or take a drink of his beer a certain way. These were all communications to me, directing me to success!

I felt so special! I was the only one Daddy trusted with this secret communication code. He always chose me because I knew the codes. I understood the secret language. So I could not wait to hear those words when teams were being chosen: "I'll take Bubba!"

It was under the shade trees throwing horseshoes that the longing I had to be chosen was fulfilled. The acknowledgment that I thirsted for was quenched. I would practice throwing horseshoes when no one else was around, just so I would be able to perform well when the time came, to make Daddy yell, "That's five!"

I didn't want to falter in those moments, those moments when I could show Daddy he made the right choice in choosing me to be on his team. I never wanted to let him down. I lived to make beer run down his arm and see the grin on his face as he bent down to retrieve his cigarette that he had dropped on the ground in excitement. That was my validation! Those were the moments I knew Daddy was proud I was his son.

Chapter 2

The Day My Father Showed Up

Looking Into the Grandstands

I played many different types of sports as a child. I loved football, basketball, and baseball the most. I not only loved to play, but I really sought out the camaraderie that came with being part of a team. I had a deep longing to be accepted by any and everyone. I found, because I was a pretty good athlete, that I could fulfill that need for acceptance through playing sports. So I played as much as I could.

One game sticks out very distinctly in my memory. It was the only football game that I can remember my daddy coming to. I was a freshman at Forsyth Central High School and we were playing Duluth High School. I was living with my mom in Forsyth County, where we lived from the time I was eight or so years old until I began my adult life.

My mom and dad were divorced when I was one year old, so living apart from Daddy was a natural thing to me. I asked Daddy to come to the game because I knew we were playing Duluth, which was where not only my Daddy lived, but it was also where he played high school football.

There were kids on the Duluth team that were the children of my daddy's best friends. So, I thought these things might persuade him to attend the game. I will never forget Daddy telling me he was coming. It was the statement that he was coming that excited me. After all, he told me many times that he was going to pick me up, or that he was going to come to one of my sporting events, but he never showed up.

Daddy telling me he was going to come to my football game did not stir my emotions, but knowing what team we were playing and who was on that team added a little more hope that Daddy would come.

I remember the whole pre-game warm-up time, I would look up into the grandstands every chance I could, to see if Daddy followed through with his promise, maybe just this once. It has been well over twenty-five years since that day and I can still sense the worth I felt when I looked up into the top right section of the grandstands, and there stood my dad.

I stood at least six inches taller that day. He showed up! He was surrounded by his friends that had kids playing for the other team. He was stranded in the section designated for the other team. But I didn't care where he chose to stand. I was so happy that he actually did what he said he was going to do.

I can still see it as plain as day in my memory. We received the football first. I was the quarterback on offense. We were around the forty yard line where I handed the ball off to one of my running backs. I handed him the ball off the left side of the offensive line. There was a hole that you could drive a transfer truck through. As soon as the running back hit that hole he was gone to the house! I remember running and jumping up and down. We had scored! We were winning!

I looked up into the grandstands and there was Daddy smiling. His shoulders were back, his face was shining, and that's when he did it. He did something I had never seen him do before. As his arms were folded across his chest, he lifted up his left arm and, with his left hand, and gave me a thumbs-up. When someone gives you a thumbs-up, it simply means good job, or everything is okay.

It was that gesture that shouted louder than any scream of excitement. It displayed something to me more than any sign or banner trailing behind a plane flying through the air.

My Daddy not only showed up, but he was proud of me!

Our team was not very good. We ended up losing that game pretty badly, if I remember correctly. But I would not take the win over that moment Daddy gave me the thumbs-up.

I had watched other parents celebrate their children's victories. For years, I watched mother after mother and father after father grab their child and lift them up in arms of excitement and pleasure. I had watched for years, parents walk off the field or court embracing their child, win or lose.

This was my moment. The time I had waited and prayed for.

What was simply a thumbs-up to most was a compilation of years and tears for me. It was my embrace. It was my "At-a-boy!" It took sixteen years but, at that moment, I didn't care. Daddy showed up and at that moment he was proud of me. Proud to be my daddy. No trophy, no winning score, no other congratulations could compare to that one gesture. It was the one time I had someone to look up at and point to in excitement. It was the one time teammates would ask me who that was giving me a thumbs-up, and I could say, "That's my Dad!"

It was a one-time event. Never before and never again would I be able to look into the grandstands and experience that feeling of acceptance and value.

However on that day, for that moment in time, I was complete. All the practicing and all the hard work was worth it. All the lonely tears dropping from eyes in rejection and disappointment were wiped away by a thumb held in the air.

The Stepfathers

It was during this time of my life that my mom was married to my third stepfather.

I would like to take a moment and make a statement. Nothing I have written or will write in this book is meant to hurt or degrade anyone. My parents did the best they could with the knowledge and the experience they had at the time. I am thankful to the stepfathers who loved my mom and her children the best they could. So, I say nothing to hurt or dishonor anyone who played major roles in my life. I mention that this was my third stepfather merely to note the instability in which I was raised.

My third stepdad was my stepdad for the longest time. He was in my life, married to my mom from the time I was eight or nine years old or so until I was twenty-one years old. He was a good man. He was trying to raise two kids who were not his own. Two kids who were full of anger, frustration, hurt, and misguided hatred.

He tried to love these two kids while raising his own daughter and son. So I am thankful for this man. I am thankful because, for the greatest portion of my life, he took us to church and showed us the love of God. For the most part, he was the only example of what a father was that I ever knew. He made some mistakes but he was the only consistent male in my life.

22

I remember he would take us to watch his son play football. His son was about four or five years younger than I was, and he lived with his mother and stepfather, as well. They lived about an hour or so from us, but when he had a football game we would load up the car and drive the hour just to watch his son play ball. I would watch my stepdad and my mom cheer for the success of his son. I would cheer him on, too. He was my brother and I wanted him to do well. I wanted him to be able to look over into the grandstands and see us, to see me cheering him on to victory. He was a great football player, so we always had a lot to cheer about.

I remember feeling like I never wanted my brother to experience what I had experienced so many times as I looked into the stands in vain.

Despite the heart I had for my brother to succeed, my stepfather never came to any of my games to cheer for me like he did for his son. I couldn't help but feel confused, hurt and rejected again and again.

What had I done to cause my stepdad not to love and support me enough to come and cheer me on?

I am not talking about a game or two over the weekend. I played two or three sports almost year round for the better part of my high school years. That's a lot of football, basketball, and baseball games, and wrestling matches. I cannot recall one game or match that my stepdad ever attended. Not one.

I never understood why he didn't come. For most of those games and matches I had no one in the stands supporting me, no one to give a thumbs-up, or to embrace me after a tough loss. I struggled with constantly feeling like I was broken. I was living out of a box built for damaged goods.

Why would we drive over an hour to cheer on my brother, but no one could drive just minutes away to offer me a bit of encouragement?

It was holidays and birthdays I hated the most.

Most of those days were nothing but disappointment for me. I remember one birthday in particular. It was the late 1980's and rap music hit our lives. Along with the music came a new type of dancing. It was called Break Dancing, and I was very good at it.

Break dancing was huge at that time in the larger cities of America. A lot of the break dancing took place on the ground. We did moves like the backspin, the head stand, the worm, or the helicopter. It was basically spinning around and around on your back or head while on the ground.

To prevent injury on concrete or grass, everyone would take cardboard boxes, cut them into pieces and lay them on the ground. We would lay the cardboard out and tape the pieces together to make a dance floor.

The other essential for break dancing was a boombox, which was a radio/cassette-tape player (replaced later by CD players) that usually had two huge speaker inside it.

Real break dancers would carry huge boomboxes on their shoulders as they bobbed up and down to the beat of the music. All I wanted for my birthday that year was the largest boombox in the whole county! I wanted something so heavy I could barely carry it. The more speakers, the better.

I remember begging my mom to buy me a boombox for my birthday. My mom was a homemaker at the time, so her only source of income was what my stepdad brought in. He was a very hard worker, as a firefighter and an EMT. So he would pull two twenty-four-hour shifts back-to-back, and then be off for twenty-four hours. So he would work forty-eight hours and only be home twenty-four hours. He had this type of a schedule for as long as I knew him.

That birthday is etched into my memory. At school, I was anticipating the time when I could get home and get my boombox. I couldn't wait to throw my boombox on my right shoulder while grasping my cardboard box under my left arm, and off I would go to break dance the evening away.

I heard Mom's car tires pressing the gravel drive way. I ran to open the door just as she pulled to a stop under the carport. She opened her door and it almost took out my leg as I ran to meet her.

"Did you get it?" I asked.

"Yes," she said!

I turned toward the back door of the car to pull the huge box out of the back seat. As I went to maneuver around Mom's open door, I noticed she turned to reach for something. She picked up a small box about twelve inches in length by eight inches in height.

This was the boombox, the present I had waited for.

I had not been able to concentrate on my assignments all day, because I couldn't wait to get home and hear my boombox blast that rap music.

I had told all my friends that I would bring it to school and show them my huge multi-speaker boombox. My boombox was sure to be bigger than theirs. It was certain to have more speakers than theirs. I could not wait to show them what a real boombox looked and sounded like.

All that came to a screeching halt when, with one arm, my Mom handed me a small, grey radio with one small speaker on the right side of it.

My heart sank.

My expectations were crushed.

My excitement was replaced with what felt like rejection, yet again.

What was I going to do?

I remember thinking: Remember what you were taught. Always be thankful for any gift you are given.

I didn't want to hurt my Mom's feelings, so I smiled and told her, Thank you so much!

I tore the box open and put four new C batteries in the back of the radio. I put the radio on my right shoulder and off I went.

I didn't make it far around the house before I collapsed in disappointment. I set the radio down and looked at it. My whole young life was staring back at me in the form of a radio with four C batteries and one speaker.

The only thing I could hear coming from the speaker was, "HAHAHAHA! You thought you would have something to brag about and show off to your buddies, but you are nothing, and have nothing to be proud of."

All my buddies had huge boomboxes that took six, eight, or even ten C batteries to power them. I couldn't show them my one-speaker radio with its four C batteries. They would make fun of me. It would validate their claims that I was poor and had nothing to brag about.

What was I going to tell the kids at school the next morning? What was I going to show the kids on the school bus? I sat there, leaning against the block walls of the house and just cried.

Every negative thing I heard about myself was true. Every negative thing I thought about my life was seemingly true. I had no father to answer the questions I was having about my boyhood - my self worth, my lack of validation. Nowhere to run. No one to listen. No guidance available. So I just sat alone and cried.

It wouldn't have been so bad, but guess what my stepsister got for her birthday!

Yep, a huge boombox that took eight D batteries to power it.

Guess what my brother pulled out of the car when he came to stay with us for summer break.

The largest boombox I had ever seen in person.

It was the boombox I always wanted, the one I was hoping for, and I was telling all my buddies I was going to get it for my birthday. This would play out birthday after birthday, Christmas after Christmas, special day after special day.

The summer between my sixth- and seventh-grade years of school was devastating for me. It was a time when most of my friends took the opportunity to validate the negative feelings I had of myself.

A kid who was a year ahead of me in school somehow came to hate me. He was a very popular guy and most kids wanted to be liked by him. Not only was he the starting quarterback, but he also came from a very prominent family in our community.

For some reason, that summer he approached my closest friends and told them that they could be in his inner circle if they would do one thing. They had to stop being my friend. They had to turn their backs on me and have no contact with me.

I know that sounds like a plot for a tv show or something, but it's true. That summer, when I would call my friends, they would not answer or return my calls. I would see them at the movie theater and they would walk right by me without saying a word to me. They wouldn't sit with me; they would sit with the other guy and their new friends.

I remember a phone conversation with a girl who had been one of my closest friends for several years. Her words to me were, "Hey, David, do me a favor. Never call or talk to me again!"

I hadn't done anything to make these kids reject me. It was all because another kid's insecurities demanded that they reject me.

This went on for a whole year. I would walk through the hallways at school and they would turn away, stick their noses up and look the other way. I am not talking about one or two acquaintances. I am talking about a dozen or more of my closest friends. I was not invited to their parties anymore, or asked to spend the night at their houses. I was living the life of a stepchild even at school.

Rejection, failure, heartache, and dysfunction were all words that described my young life. I was a stepchild living a stepchild's life.

By the time I was old enough to drive, I was pretty much accustomed to expecting the so-called short end of the stick.

I will never forget standing in the parking lot of a shopping center where my stepfather's friend was to deliver my first car to my stepfather and me. When I saw it pull in, I thought, "Please don't let this be my car."

But it was.

It was a sky blue, four-door Oldsmobile, with its paint flaking off so badly the metal showed through. The paint wasn't just fading; it was literally flaking off.

It had a crushed velvet blue interior with an old push button AM/FM radio, no cassette tape player or CD player, just an AM/FM Radio.

I looked out of the corner of my eye into the face of stepfather. He had a smirk on his face. I knew what he was thinking: "What a pile of crap!" He smiled with what looked like joy that I was getting this crappy car, as though he thought this is all I deserved. He seemed proud that he was buying me this car - not proud of the car, but proud that it was a piece of crap!

With that smile firmly implanted in my mind, I did what I always did. I suppressed my disappointment, hugged his neck, and said thank you. Then I jumped into the car and took off.

The feelings of worthlessness received another gut shot the day my stepsister got her first car. It was a two-door Camaro sports car. That blow was repeated when my stepbrother got a red sports car for his first vehicle. It was even decked out with a loud, booming sound system. And my older sister's first car was a white Mustang.

When I would drive to school, I would park in the back of the building, where the dumpsters were, and avoid everyone I could. I wanted no one to know that car was mine.

I would drive and sit real low in the seat so no one would see me driving the car. Nevertheless, I still heard people's comments and saw the stares when they didn't know I could see them. Everything seemed designed to validate every negative thing I had heard about myself, and had come to believe. I was only good enough to be a stepchild. I was not really a part of the family. I only had the privilege to take part because my stepdad was married to my mom.

I was nothing more than baggage, part of the marriage deal that couldn't be negotiated out. I was second class, the broken part of a broken family that didn't deserve the same things that the legitimate children of the house deserved. I was the kid that other parents told their children to stay away from.

And many of them did.

Chasing the Curve Ball

If you were to ask most kids when they first threw a ball with their father, they probably would respond by saying that they didn't remember. It's a fairly normal event in a young person's life for their father to do things with them, things like throwing a baseball, going fishing, maybe shopping, or teaching them to swim or ride a bike. These are all very normal events in one's life.

If you think back to your childhood, I am sure you will be able to remember one or two, or maybe more, of these events in your life. They are just things a father does. I'm sure it's written in a fathering manual somewhere that, as a father, you must interact with your children by teaching them to do these things.

While many people forget about such commonplace times spent with their dads, taking them for granted, I vividly remember the first time my dad ever threw a baseball with me. I recall it like it was yesterday because, not only was it the first time Daddy threw a baseball with me, it was the *only* time.

It was a hot, sunny day in Duluth. One of my best friends growing up and I were in the backyard of my dad's home, just around the corner of the yard from the shade trees and horseshoe pit.

Jeremy and I were killing time tossing the baseball around while we waited to do the things we had planned for later, like cruising the back roads looking for girls, eating again, fishing, hunting, and eating some more. We were young men in high school, and productive events such as working and studying were not on our radar.

Whenever we had a spare moment in between these very important events, we would throw the baseball around.

Buzzard and I – Buzzard was Jeremy's nickname - were tossing the ball around when Daddy drove up in his 1972 Chevy pickup truck. It was green and white, had a 350 four-bolt main with Corvette transmission and rally wheels. Daddy loved that truck almost as much as I did.

When he drove up and got out of the truck, he called out, "What's up, boys?" as he begin to walk to the house. I didn't even think about asking Daddy to throw with us. It was something that I had never experienced or expected.

As Daddy passed Buzzard and me, he asked, "Did I ever tell you the time I played in the Little League World Series?"

Wait… what?

My dad played baseball in the Little League World Series???

Why did I not know this? This would have been great ammunition to have in those moments on the playground when all the boys were vying over whose dad was the biggest and baddest. I could have shut every mouth on the jungle gym! I would have been the envy of all the guys if I had known and been able to brag that my dad played in the Little League World Series. I would not have had to hide behind the tire swing or quickly walk away from the swing set when others were telling stories about the successes of their hero fathers.

Then Daddy informed us that, not only did he play in the Little League World Series, he was the starting pitcher in the championship game!

ARE YOU KIDDING!!!

What?!?!?!

My daddy was a super hero and I didn't even know it!

Then Daddy dropped the bomb on us. He said, "Not only did I play in the championship game, but I was the starting pitcher."

At that moment, I didn't know if I believed him or not. I didn't even know whether I was proud of him or wanted to kill him for never telling me this before.

When other boys spoke about and bragged on their dads, I literally would slowly excuse myself from the conversation, or I would lie like a dog and make up some outlandish story about him just to impress the kids listening. This would have been something that could have kept me from retreating into my cave of thinking – though I loved him earnestly – that I had a loser dad compared to the dads of others.

I told him I didn't believe him. He assured me it was true. When he said his best pitch was a curve ball, I had to challenge him to show me if he still had it and could make the ball move.

Then it happened.

I laid down a challenge he could not walk away from. He told Buzzard to give him his glove, and after a few warm-up throws, I asked him to show me this famous curve ball.

Keep in mind, Daddy had not picked up a baseball in probably fifteen to twenty years. I didn't really expect much from this famous curve.

Daddy told me to squat down like a catcher and get my glove up in a ready position. He kicked his front leg up, shifted his hips towards me, and with his right hand cocked back he released one of the most beautiful curve balls I have ever seen.

It was like it dropped off a table.

I was amazed! I always wanted to throw a curve, but I never had anyone to teach me how. I didn't even know how to grip the ball in my hand. Now I was catching the pitch I always wanted thrown, and from the man I always wanted to throw with.

You may be asking yourself what the big deal is. Why would throwing a baseball with my dad be a big enough deal to write about? Well, I'll tell you why it is such a big deal. What makes this such a big deal is this was the first and only time my dad ever threw a baseball with me, and I was seventeen years of age! I was no longer a child. I was almost an adult before my father took the time to pick up a baseball and toss it around with me.

Something is wrong with this picture! At the time I didn't care. I didn't think of all the times he could have thrown the ball with me. He could have taught me how to hold the baseball, how to use my arm positions, how to release the ball to throw a curveball. But he chose not to.

For the first time, my dad threw me a curve and I enjoyed it.

Usually the curves Daddy threw me were in the form of broken promises, promising the moon and delivering nothing. Many times, he would promise to come and pick me up so I could spend the weekend with him. The curve would come on Friday night when I would call to ask when he was coming, only to hear, "Son, your daddy is in jail."

Or the curve he threw was that the phone would ring endlessly. No answer would be the response to let me know, yet again, Daddy had thrown his signature pitch, the curveball.

Daddy Is Trying To Live Right

My mother brought me up in church. At least three times per week, we were in a church service somewhere. Most of the times, the singing, preaching, or praying would go late into the day or night as we sought to make our way into God's presence.

A large contingent of older ladies, with long hair pulled into buns or into honeycomb-shaped ponytails on top of their heads, would be shouting and praising God. They would go throughout the church laying hands on everyone in sight as they prayed in tongues that were unknown to all in the room. They would cast devils out of people, and lead them to the altar of repentance.

Meanwhile, the men would be preaching and dancing in the Spirit all over the front of the sanctuary. This would go on for hours. I remember many times crawling under a pew and falling asleep. I loved the presence of God, but sometimes my little body just needed some rest.

I played the drums in church for many years. This was the platform God gave me to teach me how to flow with Holy Spirit's direction in a corporate setting. I remember vividly how Holy Spirit would come upon me and I would play unto Him with beats and rhythms I was never trained to play.

35

As I sat behind the drum set, often behind or inside a drum screen, Holy Spirit taught me to hear His voice. I would sense when to play louder or softer, when to close a song and begin another. I loved helping set the atmosphere for the minister to speak and for God to move.

The first time I was scheduled to play the drums during a Sunday evening service, I couldn't wait to tell Daddy. We went to eat after the morning service and, after eating, we found a pay phone and I called Daddy.

In case you're unfamiliar with pay phones, they were stationary, public phones located throughout most towns and cities, hanging inside of phone booths or on the side of retail buildings. We didn't have cell phones, pagers, or car phones back in those days. So, if you were away from home or not close to a land line, the only way to communicate over a significant distance was by pay phones. At that time, a local call cost a quarter to talk for five minutes.

Anyway, we called Daddy and I remember telling him I was going to be playing the drums at service that night and asking if he might be able to come. He said he was happy that I was playing the drums and going to church, and he told me he would try his best to come to service that evening.

I was ecstatic! Not only was I going to play the drums during a real service, but my dad was coming to church! As excited as I was that he was coming to hear me play the drums, I was more excited that maybe Daddy would hear about Jesus and give his life to Him.

Once I got off the phone, I remember Momma asking me what Daddy said. Overjoyed, I told her, "He said he was going to come to service tonight!"

I was so happy! To a ten- or eleven-year-old boy who loved his daddy and wanted nothing more than to make him proud, this news was life changing.

Momma didn't have the same reaction. Her response was, "Son, don't get your hopes up. Your daddy probably will not show up."

What?! Why would you say that, I thought to myself. I got mad at my mother, thinking maybe she was just jealous that I was so excited to see my dad. Maybe she didn't want Daddy to come and see me play because she didn't like him.

I immediately defended my dad and was upset at my mom, thinking she was coming against Daddy. I know now that she was simply trying to lower the fall zone from which I was almost certain to drop. She was trying to protect my young heart. She had been there many times when Daddy didn't show up in my life, and she simply didn't want me to get hurt yet again. I couldn't see that then.

To make a long story short, after practicing with the choir I headed straight to the front parking lot and waited for Daddy. Once the other kids noticed that I was not running around playing with them, they came and asked what was wrong with me. I shared with them that nothing was wrong; I was just waiting on my dad to show up for service. I wanted to be the first person he saw on entering the parking area. I wanted to feel him wrap me in his arms and to hear the words I had never heard him say to me before, "Son I am so proud of you."

Well, I waited as long as I could. Maybe he was running late, I thought. Maybe he had to stop for gas, or grab me a gift for my big moment. So I went ahead and manned my station at the drum set with the expectation that, as I played, I would see Daddy enter the sanctuary to the cadence of the drums his little boy was playing.

As I played, I kept my eye on the back entrance. One song ended and another began, as we played wholeheartedly through our song list. I watched as Momma smiled at me with tears of bliss in her eyes. I noticed the pastor clapping his hands to the drumbeat as he and I worshiped the Lord together. I saw my friends, church mothers, deacons, and Sunday school teachers watching me with faces full of acceptance and cheer as I played those drums with all my might.

The worship portion of the service ended and, even though everyone in the sanctuary was so encouraging and happy for me, their love could not fill the emptiness that only my Daddy could have filled.

I smiled and lowered my head as I walked away from the stage area. I whispered to Mom that I was going to the restroom to relieve myself. She thought by relieving myself I was saying I had to use the restroom, but I was about to burst open with sadness and emotions that tried to pour out of me. I don't remember if I made it to the restroom or just went outside. This event would play over and over so many times in my life that it's hard for me to keep the details separate from one time to the next.

I don't even think I came back into service. The first major church event in my life ended with me having a broken heart and dealing with the old question of why I was not good enough for my own dad to come and support me.

It was several years later that my prayers were answered. I was full of joy that my sister and stepmother were attending church with us, because of the change that was taking place in their lives. But on this particular Sunday, something else happened: Daddy showed up at church.

I was about sixteen years old at this time, and was still playing the drums for our church. Seeing my daddy sitting in the audience that morning brought me so much joy and happiness that years of hurt seemed to melt away in just that moment.

I can't recall much about the service other than my dad answered the altar call that morning to receive Jesus as his Savior. I was so happy! I had prayed for this day for so long!

Over the next several weeks I watched as Daddy tried to live for the Lord. I grew up in a church atmosphere that was very holiness driven. Now don't misunderstand me, I believe there is a lifestyle that we must live to correctly portray the name of Jesus to this world. I believe in a standard of living that separates Christians from the rest of the world.

I also believe that there is nothing we can do outside of repenting of our sins and asking for Jesus' forgiveness that will make us acceptable to the Father. The moment we turn our hearts to Jesus and truly repent of our sins, we are made acceptable to Him. This was not taught in our church. We were taught forgiveness was a free gift but staying forgiven took work. A lot of work!

I watched my dad work to change his life. I watched him try to stop a thirty-plus-year smoking addiction in a moment. He tried to break a thirty-plus-year alcohol addiction in the same moment. Of course he had to find a new occupation, a whole new group of friends, construct a new way of life, and also go apologize and make right everyone he had ever let down.

I stood back and watched as Daddy tried to be pleasing to His Father. And try he did. I saw Daddy chew gum for the first time in my life so he could alleviate the craving of nicotine. He tried to isolate himself at home a lot, to try and avoid the temptations that were lurking around every corner.

Daddy loved God. He wanted to please God. However my daddy was broken. He was a middle-aged man crippled by addictions and failure, haunted by years of lying, scamming, cheating, and living life as hard as he could. He had no training or discipleship to fall back on.

Daddy didn't understand the meaning of spiritual warfare, or demonic influences, or ungodly soul ties. He was introduced to a Savior that loved him enough to give His life for him, and my dad was willing to do anything he could to earn this love and forgiveness.

However, Daddy soon found out the love His heavenly Father was offering could not be earned or lived.

It wasn't long until Daddy was back to the only life he knew. It didn't take but a couple of weeks for Daddy to realize he couldn't please a Father he didn't even know. I look back now and I realize that, in those few short weeks, I was really watching my dad live out my life.

My whole life I was lived trying to please a daddy that I really didn't even know.

I knew who he was a couple of weekends a year. I knew who I saw on holidays and an occasional run-in at Ted's Fruit Stand. The truth is, I was trying to love an image of a man that I gathered from other people's opinions of who Daddy was. I didn't really know who my daddy was. Was he the man that ran out on me as a one-year-old child? Was he the man who gave me the thumbs-up at the football game? Was he the alcoholic promise-breaker that had left me standing outside the church waiting for him to arrive? Or was he the man who would cry at the drop of a hat when you asked him about Jesus or the Bible?

I didn't know who my daddy really was, and I am not sure anyone did. But this one thing I know: there was a time he had an encounter with his heavenly Father, and it was very meaningful to him. Maybe, just maybe, he tried to live up to the expectations people put on him, and because he didn't really know this Father, he gave up on a relationship that he never really had to work for to begin with!

Just a' Swingin'

There was a very popular country and western song that would play on the radio when I was a kid. It was about a young boy and girl who lived in the same neighborhood. They would sit and swing on the front porch of their house and that's where they began to fall in love. Later, after they married, they would sit on their front porch and just swing.

It was on a front porch swing where I had one of the worst, and later, greatest moments of my life.

I had spoken to Daddy earlier in the week and asked if I could come spend the weekend with him. He said yes and that he would come pick me up on Friday.

You can imagine my excitement. All week I turned down invitations to spend the weekend with my friends. I didn't go to the skating rink, I didn't want to ride my three-wheeler, and even the fact that my stepbrother was coming to visit did not persuade me to stay home that weekend.

I came home from school on Friday, after what seemed to be the longest day in history. I went straight to my room and packed my bag to spend the weekend with Daddy. It must have been around 4:00 or 5:00 o'clock in the evening when I first went out to sit on the front porch swing and wait for Daddy.

I remember the other kids playing out in the yard and asking me if I wanted to come play in the woods. I told them no because Daddy was coming to get me at any time. I was afraid if I went out in the woods to play and Daddy came to get me, he would leave if I wasn't waiting on him. So I just sat on that front porch swing and I swang.

It was fairly late in the evening when I heard the front door squeak as it opened. It was Momma. I will never forget what she said and the look on her face. I heard the brokenness in her voice that surely came from knowing that what she was about to say was going to once again break the heart of her son.

Momma asked me to come inside. I told her no, I was waiting on Daddy. It was probably around 9:00 or 10:00pm by this time. I had sat there all evening, just swinging and waiting anxiously for Daddy.

She sat down on the swing with me, put her arm around me and said, "Son, your daddy isn't coming."

It would be years later - I was twenty-seven years old, married, and pastoring my first church - before I would ever realize the impact that those words would have on me.

The church was named The ROCK of Dahlonega. It was located in the mountains of North Georgia.

We were in the worship portion of the service that day and the Spirit of God was moving very strong. I was standing on the front row beside my beautiful wife, worshiping the Lord with both of my hands raised as high as I could lift them.

Suddenly, Holy Spirit reminded me of that day I sat on the front porch in the swing and waited for Daddy. I told the Lord I remembered that day. As real as the sun in the sky, I heard Holy Spirit say, "The day your daddy didn't show up is the day your Father did."

I will never forget that moment as long as I live.

The Lord told me He showed up that day. That He was there swinging with me on that front porch.

I wasn't swinging alone.

Until my mom came out to tell me my dad was not coming to pick me up, I felt all alone. But it was at that very time when my Father took my daddy's place.

It took my dad not showing up to open a place for my Father to show up.

That day I thought I was just swinging, but in reality, I was resting in the arms of my Father.

Chapter 3

Talking to a Tombstone

Texas Trip

I was eighteen years old at this time. I had family members that lived in Texas that we had not seen in a few years. Daddy just decided one afternoon to go and visit them.

It was a fourteen-hour drive from Daddy's house to my Aunt Polly's house in Midlothian, Texas. Long road trips like this one can take families several weeks or months to plan out. But not my dad. This is the way he lived life. He was a fly-by-the-seat-of-your-pants type of guy. He lived life to the fullest. No shoes, no shirt, no plans, no problem for him.

Daddy approached me earlier in the day and said he was going to Texas, and wanted to know if I wanted to join him on the adventure. I was like, absolutely!

A week with my dad, traveling the highways of America - that was the kind of trip I had long dreamed of. It had only taken eighteen years to come to pass, but it really didn't matter to me.

We met at a friend of Daddy's about 8:00pm, since he had to close a couple of deals before leaving. Daddy's deals were not like the deals most fathers close before a big family trip. The loose ends Daddy had to tie up were a lot more secretive. He wasn't closing on the sale of a car or house, finalizing an analytical report for his company, or finishing up a painting or flooring job. These are things most fathers would be doing prior to setting out on a week-long vacation to another state. Not my dad!

The important business that Daddy had to finish up before we could leave was the very important job of cutting the new shipment of methamphetamines that he and his business partner just received.

You see, that's how you make your money when dealing in things like illegal drugs. You pay for a certain amount of dope, then you cut out a portion of the pure dope and add an undetectable agent to the rest. You then have more dope than what you bought, so you have more profit.

I am only sharing this so that you can understand the mindset behind almost every decision my father made. Every decision he made was based on his personal wants and needs, his habits and addictions, and what would best fit the moment. We couldn't leave until 9:00 or 10:00 o'clock to set out on a fourteen-hour drive because my dad had to cut and sell drugs before we left.

These were very common things for me to see. I grew up seeing them cut meth. It was common to see beautiful women - old and young, alike - go into the bathroom and shoot up dope. It was an almost everyday event to walk into a room and be greeted by naked women looking for their next fix, women so high on drugs that they would at times invite two, three, or four men to engage in illicit sexual activities. Things most people only see in movies or on television shows I saw commonly.

These were not isolated events taking place; they were part of the lifestyle my daddy's friends lived. He was the ring leader, the man in charge. My dad made his living supplying people with their drugs of choice. He had the money, the power, the fame, and could get almost anything he wanted any time he asked for it. To some, this would be the height (or depths, as you know) of life, but to me this was just normal.

Late that Friday night, Daddy and I set out on our road trip to Texas. He wanted to lead off driving. I tried to tell him I could drive, but he insisted on driving. This was the way he thought. He had an eighteen-year-old son who was perfectly legal and capable of driving, but instead, he wanted to drive after drinking all day – not to mention the fact that he had not had a valid driver's license in over twenty years!

What made him think this was a reasonable, sensible idea?

Regardless of how little sense it made, that was Daddy. That's the way he thought.

The reason for me telling about this trip to Texas is mainly about this one event.

As we were about to pull out of the driveway, Daddy, who did not do drugs, pulled out a small bag with powder inside. I knew exactly what it was. It was an eight-ball of meth. What I didn't know is why Daddy was pulling it out of his pocket.

Like I said previously, Daddy was not one to use drugs. As a matter of fact, he always told me very emphatically to NEVER do drugs. He didn't mind me drinking cold beer, and would even give me a couple if I asked, but he was adamant that I stay away from consuming drugs.

So I was a little perplexed when he pulled the meth out of his pocket and stuck his Old Timer pocket knife into the meth. He shook what remained on the blade into his mouth. I was a little surprised, but it didn't really rattle me. What happened next, though, shook me to my core.

Daddy looked over at me and said, "We have a long drive ahead of us. Do you want some to help up stay up for the trip?"

I laughed and said, "No, I have never tried a drug, so I am not going to start now."

At that time in my life I really had never tried any type of drug. I had drunk alcohol a few times at parties, or when challenged by friends. But I thought it was ironic that the very first time I was ever offered a hard drug like meth, it was being offered by my own father. The one who instilled in me a desire to avoid drugs was now offering them to me.

Several times over the next few days, I had difficulty dealing with what had happened in that black Cutlass Supreme.

Why would Daddy offer me something that he always warned me against? Why, all of a sudden, would Daddy want me to use a drug that I watched every day destroy people's lives?

The trip to Texas was a dream. It was so fun meeting family members that I had not met before. It was full of love, laughter, and new experiences. Daddy and I had a wonderful time together. I saw New Orleans and Dallas for the first time. We went and toured the place where JFK was supposedly murdered. It was a wonderful time!

But in the quiet moments, just before my eyes would close to rest, I couldn't help but try and come to grips with why my dad would want me use meth. Didn't he love me enough to want to protect me? I didn't understand, and to this day, I still don't understand. I guess it is one of those things that happen while living with such a broken person.

Marital Advice

My girlfriend and I drove up the driveway where my daddy spent most of his time. It was the home of a man named Everett. He was daddy's "business partner," a very mean grumpy old man who was an alcoholic, as well. He was very successful in business, owning a grading company and several dump trucks.

However, he was one of the meanest men I had ever met. His drink of choice was vodka, and the more he drank, the meaner he would become. I had heard him curse people out to the point they would leave his home in tears. I watched him mistreat people and mishandle women until, often times, I would jump in and distract him away from them. He knew not to mess with me because, number one, I would kick a mudhole in his butt, and, number two, he was very scared of my daddy.

I was very hesitant to take my girlfriend over to Everett's house, but I had to let Daddy know the good news.

We pulled up the driveway and Daddy was standing outside, leaning on the railing overlooking the back yard where all the trucks were parked. He was happy to see Stephanie and me, and asked what we were up to and how things were going.

We told him it was good and I asked if I could talk to him alone for a second. I didn't want Stephanie to be with us, because I never knew what Daddy was going to say. So there Daddy and I stood, alone, leaned up on the porch railing. Daddy asked me what was up and I told him.

"Daddy," I said, "Stephanie and I are getting married!" He was very excited because he really liked Stephanie and told me many times that she was a keeper.

It might sound odd that I was kind of looking for some fatherly advice about marriage. I mean, in my mind I knew he could not offer me any advice when it came to marriage or how to treat women. But I think, as a son, I longed for Daddy's approval.

There was an awkward silence for a minute, and then Daddy finally inhaled to make a comment. Here it was, the moment of validation from my hero. It was finally the moment when Daddy could lead me with some constructive criticism, some guiding wisdom, or maybe a little careful knowledge. This was the time. Here was the moment.

Daddy put his arm around me with his right hand gripping my right shoulder and said, "Son, always make sure things are taken care of at home, and then you can get you a little on the side."

And there it was.

That was the marital advice my father gave me when I told him I was marrying the love of my life. He didn't instruct me with wisdom that would arm me as we marched forward into the hardest relationship to maintain in a human's life time. He gave me no words to encourage me to choose Stephanie every day and to forsake all others in my care for her. He offered no scripture references.

The fatherly advice to me was to "take care of things at home…" before I went out and had sex with other women!

It still makes me grin to this day. Not a grin of appreciation. Not a grin of anticipation or excitement. I grin as I think how much I love my daddy despite how warped his view of sex and marriage really was.

I watched for years as my dad mistreated women, my stepmother, in particular. My stepmother was - and is - as close to a saint as I could ever imagine. She was married to my dad all my childhood and teenage life. She was the only stable thing my sisters and I had in our lives with Daddy.

In spite of the fact that Daddy treated her terribly, she stayed with him. I look back now and I am saddened as I think how lonely and rejected she must have felt for so many years. Daddy would stay gone days at a time, doing who-knows-what with who-knows-who. And there my stepmother would be, raising her daughter and loving me and my sister when we came to visit.

She never treated us like stepchildren. She always loved us and gave us sound and wise direction. How can people treat others like Daddy treated her? I don't understand. I thank God that Betsy, my stepmother, was in my life!

I hate that my daddy didn't see what an incredible woman he had or treat her as the queen she was!

I think, seeing how Daddy and all these other knuckle-headed men treated their wives and girlfriends taught me how I *didn't* want to treat women.

I have never taken my Daddy's advice. I made a vow to my wife Stephanie on August 19, 1995, and to this day, I have kept my vow to her. I have forsaken all others and I have cleaved to my wife.

No one is more important to me than she is. She doesn't have to worry about me "getting a little on the side." She is my one and only. She is my gift from God. The Bible says, *"When a man finds a wife, he finds a good thing."* (Proverbs 18:22)

I found my good thing many years ago and I thank God I had a dad that showed me how I was NOT to treat her.

That's My Boy!

County Line Baptist Church was where I was attending service one Sunday morning when I felt very impressed to go visit my dad.

It was beyond a feeling. I knew the Lord was trying to tell me something. I was alone at church that morning because Stephanie was at home sick. It was very unusual that I went to church alone, because Stephanie and I never missed a church service. But she was under the weather, so I went on to church by myself. As I sat there in service, I could not shake the feeling that I needed to go see my dad.

By this time, Stephanie and I had been married for a little over a year, and Daddy had been diagnosed with cancer. He was eaten up with cancer.

The doctors had given him just a few months to live. I had not seen Daddy in several weeks. I just couldn't pull myself together enough to go see him. The last time I saw Daddy several weeks earlier, I took him to get his head shaved. He had lost a lot of weight, and by this time, they had placed him in a cancer hospice. I told the Lord I would go see Daddy, but I didn't know where the hospice was. I didn't even know the name of the place.

I called Stephanie after service and told her I was going to go visit Daddy. I had no address, no name of the facility, no contact information. All I knew was, it was in Atlanta somewhere.

So, off I went. I drove down the highway to Atlanta. I came upon a road that I felt impressed to exit the Interstate. It was called North Druid Hills. I wasn't sure if I had overheard my sisters mention that particular road, or if Holy Spirit was telling me to exit, but I exited.

I saw a gas station across the Interstate on the right-hand side of the road, and thought I could stop there and look through the phone book that was chained to payphone. I pulled into the gas station and walked to the payphone booth and - wouldn't you know it - someone had ripped most of the phone book out.

About that time, a man walked out of the store. I knew I was supposed to ask this man if he knew where the cancer hospice was I was looking for.

I walked up to the gentleman and I asked, "Sir, I know you don't know me and I don't know you, either, but my dad is in a cancer hospice somewhere in Atlanta and I am trying to find him. You wouldn't happen to know where there is a cancer hospice close by, do you?"

The man looked at me with a puzzled look and said, "Yes, (he pointed back across the Interstate) the place you're looking for is that building right over there."

He told me to cross back over the Interstate and take my first right-hand turn. The building I was looking for would be the first building on the left. I was less than a quarter of a mile from the facility! Holy Spirit had led me straight to the place I needed to be!

After parking, I hesitantly walked into the facility, still not one-hundred percent sure that I had found the correct place. I walked up to the nurses' station and asked if they had a John David Edmondson as a patient there. They told me they did and pointed to the second or third room on the left.

As I turned to walk to the room I was overwhelmed with emotion: excitement, anticipation, fear, regret, sadness, and so many more feelings all rushed together.

What would Daddy look like? What would he say to me? Would he be happy to see me or wonder why I haven't came to see him sooner?

I walked slowly to the door and saw the back of what looked to be a one-hundred-year-old man.

I was taken back, to the point that I looked again at the name tag hanging outside the door. The name on the sign was Edmondson. This was Daddy's room.

About the time I was about to turn and walk away from the sight that I was not prepared to see, I noticed a nurse on the other side of the bed stick her head up and smile at me. Then my feeble, weak Daddy turned his head and looked at me.

Here was the moment I anticipated and feared all at the same time. Daddy saw me. What was going to be his reaction? How would he respond?

When Daddy saw me, he smiled and turned to the nurse and with a pride in his eyes I had never seen before, he said to the nurse, "That's my boy."

Three words destroyed years of built up hurt, rejection, pain, and resentment. Three little words spoken in a fleeting moment filled every hole in a heart that was shattered by a thousand broken promises.

"That's my boy," is all he could gather the strength to say.

The look in his eye held more validation than a hundred novels on love could describe. My daddy did love me. He was proud of me. I was his boy!

I walked over to the bed and he stretched his hand out to me. I took his feeble, cold hand in mine and gently squeezed it in an attempt to return the validation he had just extended to me.

I said, "Hey, Daddy. How are you doing, Buddy?"

And he tried to mumble something to me. The nurse looked at me and whispered to tell me that he could hear and understand, but he was having trouble forming his words and sentences. I smiled and nodded at her, and began to talk to my daddy as if we were sitting out under the shade trees, throwing horseshoes again.

The nurse left, and there I was, alone with my Superman, who looked more like Skeletor.

Daddy weighed about 100 pounds. He was always larger than life. He was always so strong, courageous, and a man no one wanted to mess with. But as he lay there in that bed, I think he and I both came to the realization that there is always someone or something that is stronger than we are.

I sat and talked to Daddy for several minutes. I would bring up funny stories and good times we experienced together and he would smile and mumble right along. We engaged in conversation we should have had a long time earlier and more times over. However, I knew why I was there. I knew I had to make sure my daddy was ready to stand before God. I knew this was why God had told me to come, and why He led me all the way to Daddy's bedside.

The room got quiet and Daddy began to get tired. I told him I was going to go home, but I would be back in a day or two. He smiled and with tears running out of his eyes onto the pillow beneath his head, he smiled and nodded his head. I asked him, before I left, if I could ask him one question.

He nodded his head, yes.

So I mustered up all the courage I had and I asked, "Daddy are you ready to stand before the Lord? Are you right with God?"

With tears running down his face and a huge smile on his face, he nodded his head to say, yes. And as clear as a bell he said, "Yes, I am ready."

Unbeknownst to me, my sisters had just left a few minutes before I arrived, and they had prayed with Daddy to receive Jesus into His heart as his Lord and Savior.

I saw a peaceful smile that I had never seen on my Daddy's face in all my years. Over the next several days, we would be called to the hospice several times because they were sure Daddy was taking his last breath. But he would hang on and just mumble himself through another day.

The last time I saw my daddy alive was the night Stephanie and I were called down to the hospice. I knew that the Lord wanted me to pray over Daddy, anoint him for his burial, and release Daddy to the Father.

This is what the woman with the alabaster box did to Jesus just before His crucifixion. I remember anointing my daddy with some oil that I had brought with me. I laid my hands on him and prayed over him. I told Daddy that we released him from this earth, to be at peace, and go on to be with the Lord.

Stephanie and I wept, but the room was filled with peace. I was releasing my daddy, but I was surrounded by comfort and love. We were so sad, but just happy at the same time.

It was about 3:00 or 4:00 o'clock the next morning when I received the call. Daddy had passed on to Glory.

I hung the phone up, told Stephanie Daddy was gone, and turned over and went back to sleep knowing that my Daddy was safe and that I was his boy.

My Inheritance

The Bible says in Proverbs 13:22, "*A good man leaves an inheritance to his children's children.*" This is something I am striving for and believing God for: the ability to leave my children and grandchildren a great inheritance.

When Stephanie and I were first married, we truly had nothing. We purchased a small single-wide trailer from her aunt. It was twelve feet by sixty feet. It had wood siding and a shingled roof. It sat on about an acre of land. You could not have told us it was not a castle. We thought we were living high on the hog!

I would get out and cut my grass, or really my weeds, like I was cutting the grass of a mansion. One year, instead of going on vacation, we decided to put in a swimming pool. So we purchased a twenty-four-foot round, above-ground swimming pool to put up out back.

Man, please! We were living!

Stephanie and I worked hard over the next several years. We were always faithful to give the Lord our tithes first, and we were also faithful in honoring Him with offerings. The Lord has always been faithful to us, to bless us in whatever we set out to do.

There were times when we could not go out and eat with friends, or when we had to purchase used vehicles while others bought new ones. We lived in mobile homes, Stephanie's parents' home, and apartment buildings, but we were always proud of what we had and honored the Lord with what we had.

I think one driving force behind my work ethic is that desire to bless my children and grandchildren. I don't want them to struggle like Stephanie and I had to struggle. I want to leave them something more than what my daddy left me.

After Daddy passed on to Heaven, there was no inheritance to fight over. We didn't have to sit down with a lawyer and read his will and disperse all of Daddy's valuables. There was nothing to disperse.

I went to my grandmother's house and collected Daddy's things. He had a small light blue suitcase that when opened consisted of approximately three pairs of underwear and a couple of undershirts. If I remember correctly, there were a few pairs of socks, as well.

This was all Daddy had left to us, no financial inheritance, no land to pass down, no homes that we didn't build. Not one knife, gun, hat, car, or even money to pay for his own funeral or burial.

Daddy's life's worth was contained in a small, light blue suitcase. This is what he left me. This is one of the things that drive me to accomplish great things while I am on this earth. I want to leave my children more than what could fit in a small, light blue suitcase.

People make comments all the time about the things Stephanie and I have and where we live. They make comments that preachers shouldn't have nice things, nice cars, nice homes, or money in the bank. My thoughts always go back to that small, light blue suitcase, and the fact that that was all my natural daddy gave me in this life.

There is no way you can make me believe that that is acceptable to my heavenly Father! There is no way I will believe that my heavenly Father wants me to struggle through life and barely scrape by. My natural father was a sinner of sinners. He was a womanizer, a vagabond, a liar, a thief, and a con artist, and he left me nothing.
My heavenly Father is totally opposite of who my daddy was, so His desire to give me a great inheritance must be His heart for me! I will not settle, I will not accept that my only inheritance on this earth was to be a few pairs of underwear, a couple of undershirts, and a few pairs of socks! That's what Daddy left me, but that is not what my Father has purposed for me to have!

Daddy put a drive in me to work hard, honor God, love my family, and chase my dreams the day I left my MawMaw's house carrying nothing but a light blue suitcase.

Talking to a Tombstone

Daddy passed on to Glory, and because of the life he lived he left nothing for us to pay for his funeral and burial expenses.

My stepmother helped Stephanie and me pay for the funeral, but the tombstone was left up to us. I contacted a man that went to church with us at the time, who owned a memorial company, and he helped us make a headstone for Daddy's gravesite. It was simple. It had his name and a racecar with the number 3 on it. This was the number of Daddy's favorite racecar driver ever: Dale Earnhardt.

A couple of years after I had Daddy's tombstone placed at his grave, I was praying when the Lord told me to go to Daddy's grave and forgive him, and ask him to forgive me.

I thought, Wait just a minute, Lord! I can understand that I need to forgive Daddy, but why should I ask him to forgive me? Plus, he had passed on to Heaven and I couldn't get a response from him, anyway.

Holy Spirit would not let up on me. He showed me how I had a lot of hidden, built-up emotion tied to my unforgiveness toward my dad. He also revealed to me that forgiveness is hardly ever a one-way street. Like me, you can probably understand and justify why I had every right to hold unforgiveness towards my dad. All the times he made promises and didn't follow through, the things he exposed me to, the tainted wisdom he instilled in me - all these are justification for me to harbor unforgiveness.

However, I submit to you that there is never a time when unforgiveness is justified or acceptable to God.

The Lord told me to go to Daddy's grave and repent to him for holding anger, resentment, and unforgiveness toward him. He told me to tell my dad that I release him from any wrong doing, that I forgive him, and to ask him to forgive me.

So there I stood at Daddy's grave, no one around but me and a bunch of dead bodies. (I kind of felt like I was preaching in some of the churches I have ministered at since.)

I stood there for a minute and my attitude was one of, "Well I guess I'll say what I need to say, so God will be pleased with me." I was just going to go through the motions and hope God would bless me for my obedience, instead of demanding true sacrifice.

However, the moment I opened my mouth it felt like Daddy was standing right in front of me. As I gazed onto Daddy's tombstone, emotion began to flow from the depths of my soul.

I told Daddy that I was sorry for holding any ill feelings toward him. With tears running down my face, I told him that I understood that he was broken and didn't know how to show me that he loved me.

As I spoke, I could feel the layers of ungodly weights falling from my shoulders. I told Daddy that I released him from anything that I could hold against him, and asked him to please forgive me for holding on to anger and unforgiveness.

One of the greatest healing moments to ever take place in my life happened that day as I talked to a tombstone.

The Word of God teaches us that forgiveness and repentance work hand and hand. You cannot have one without the other.

Jesus said it like this, in Mark 11:25, "*And whenever you stand praying, forgive, if you have anything against anyone, so that your Father also who is in Heaven may forgive you your trespasses.*"

Again, in Colossians 3:13: "*Bearing with one another and, if one has a complaint against another, forgiving each other; as the Lord has forgiven you, so you also must forgive.*"

We embrace the part where people have to repent to us, but we naturally resist the need to forgive those same people and repent to them as well. We justify our hatred. We build fortified walls around our reasons to hold on to our anger and resentment. We hold on to these things and mask them behind empty statements like, "Well, I'll forgive, but I will not forget."

Can I submit to you that true repentance requires you to forget the trespass that was made against you?

Jesus taught the disciples to pray and added "*forgive us of our trespasses AS we forgive those who trespass against us.*"

Also the scripture that I included in the paragraph above suggests that forgiveness is a spiritual event. The Bible also suggests that we have to forgive like God forgives. God is omniscient, or all-knowing. He is also all-powerful, but in all His wisdom and power, He cannot remember a sin that He has forgiven!

When we forgive someone, it releases us from their control and from every evil soul-tie that they may have had with us.

When you forgive someone, you cut off their power to control you. However, when we hold on to unforgiveness, we are giving the major control of our lives to those same people that hurt and mistreated us in the first place.

You may feel fulfilled and justified by hating someone who hurt or mistreated you, but what that hate does is to give that person or those people the power to continue to hurt you, and ultimately determine your destiny.

Don't ever give anyone that much power over your life! Take back your authority! Take back your Peace! Take back your life!!!!!!

How you MUST forgive everyone who has wronged you, and release them from your life emotionally!

Many people in the world today - maybe even you - are being controlled by dead people. People who hurt you as a child are still victimizing you today. They are dead and gone, but through your unforgiveness, you give them access to your life.

Right now, by faith, you need to forgive those who hurt you! If they are alive, then contact them and let them know you forgive and release them. Ask them to forgive you!

If they are not alive, then, by faith, talk to their tombstone! Allow their name to come to your mind. Maybe you can imagine their face(s), as hard as it may be, and FORGIVE THEM! Not for them but for you!

Today, when I think of my Daddy, joy comes to my heart. I love my Daddy! He is resting in the presence of God right now, and I rejoice in that fact.

I can't wait to experience eternal life with Daddy. I look forward to being loved by my daddy because he will finally be able to express his love to me, since he is eternally complete and whole.

I don't hold any ill will toward him. He did the best he could in the broken, addicted state in which he lived. God has forgiven and forgotten all of Daddy's faults, so who am I to try and dig them back up again. I am free to love my wife, kids, and other important people in my life, all because one day I was willing to talk to a tombstone.

I challenge you to do the same!

Second Half Summary

Chapter 4

The Story Is All About the Daddy, Not the Son

I want to transition from telling stories and creating an image for you of my natural daddy, to revealing to you the true attributes of our heavenly Father.

Most people today have a very distorted image of God, when viewing Him as their Father.

Most of these distorted views come from bad theology and fleshly doctrine. We have been trained to see God as this huge image that resides in Heaven, Who is continually looking down on us, just waiting for us to fail or mess up so He can judge us and strike us with sickness and grief.

This image could not be further from the truth! In the following chapters we will see from one simple parable the true nature of our Father.

I would like to begin by focusing on a parable Jesus shares in the book of Luke, chapter 15 verses 11-32. It states, *"And He said, 'A man had two sons. The younger of them said to his father, 'Father, give me the share of the estate that falls to me.' So he divided his wealth between them. And not many days later, the younger son gathered everything together and went on a journey into a distant country, and there he squandered his estate with loose living. Now when he had spent everything, a severe famine occurred in that country, and he began to be impoverished. So he went and* hired himself out to one of the citizens of that country, and he sent him into his fields to feed swine. And he would have gladly filled his stomach with the pods that the swine were eating, and no one was giving anything to him. But when he came to his senses, he said, 'How many of my father's hired men have more than enough bread, but I am dying here with hunger! I will get up and go to my father, and will say to him, "Father, I have sinned against Heaven, and in your sight; I am no longer worthy to be called your son; make me as one of your hired men."' So he got up and came to his father. But while he was still a long way off, his father saw him and felt compassion for him, and ran and embraced him and kissed him. And the son said to him, 'Father, I have sinned against Heaven and in your sight; I am no longer worthy to be called your son.' But the father said to his slaves, 'Quickly bring out the best robe and put it on him, and put a ring on his hand and sandals on his feet; and bring the fattened calf, kill it, and let us eat and celebrate; for this son of mine was dead and has come to life again; he was lost and has been found.' And they began to celebrate. Now his older son was in the field, and when he came and approached the house, he heard music and dancing. And he summoned one of the servants and began inquiring what these things could be. And he said to him, 'Your brother has come, and your father has killed the fattened calf because he has received him back safe and sound.' But he became angry and was not willing to go in; and his father came out and began pleading with him. But he answered and said to his father, 'Look! For so many years I have been serving you and I have never neglected a command of yours; and yet you have never given me a young goat, so that I might celebrate with my friends; but when this son of yours came, who has devoured your wealth with prostitutes, you killed the fattened calf for him.' And he said to him, 'Son, you have always been with me, and all that is mine is yours. But we had to celebrate and rejoice, for this *brother of yours was dead and has begun to live, and was lost and has been found.'"*

It happened to be several years ago, as I was preparing to minister to a group of pastors at a conference in Virginia, that Holy Spirit revealed something to me about this parable. Holy Spirit asked me which person was the focal point in this parable.

Well, I naturally thought it was the son who received his inheritance from his dad and spent all of it. Then he came back to his father and repented for his actions. Every sermon I had ever heard drawn from this parable focused on the son. Most every Bible has a caption describing this scripture reference that focuses on the son. They read, "The prodigal son."

Every revelation I knew about this parable revealed something from the son's perspective. However, my whole view of this parable changed that day when Holy Spirit showed me the whole story revolved around the dad and not the son.

It's amazing that we only see this parable from the perspective of the son when the very first statement in the parable reads, "A MAN had two sons." So the parable Jesus begins to tell hinges on a MAN that had two sons, not the two sons. This is important because Jesus was trying to reveal the nature of the Father. The only way we can really grasp the nature of the Father through this parable is to read the events described in the parable from the perspective of the man in the story.

A Father Provides an Inheritance

One of the most eye-opening details found in the parable that Jesus tells in Luke 15 is the fact that the father in the parable provided an inheritance for his family.

Most of the parables that Jesus told were used to describe the Kingdom of Heaven, which Jesus came and reestablished on Earth. I know that a lot of the sermons we have heard preached on these parables always relate them to the "Sweet by and by," or in other words, eternity. However, that is not the Kingdom or the time frame that Jesus is describing.

We have to read this parable within the context in which Jesus spoke. The Pharisees and scribes came to Jesus complaining about His spending time with sinners and eating dinner with them. Dining with someone in those days was a high honor; it showed covenant, and was reserved for family members and close friends, most of the time.

So, for Jesus to break bread with known sinners reflected poorly on the sect that He represented, which was the church of the Jews, and therefore, it offended the Pharisees.

The context from which Jesus tells this parable was that of revealing the Kingdom of Heaven that He was establishing on earth.

Jesus is not describing Heaven. He is not revealing attributes of the eternal Kingdom of God *in* Heaven. So we must read this parable from the context of Jesus revealing to the Scribes and Pharisees, as well as the New Testament church, the attributes of the Kingdom of Heaven *on Earth*, and the qualities of God and Jesus Himself.

So when the parable begins with, "A certain man had two sons…" we can relate that certain man to God, or Jesus, and his sons, to Christians or believers.

Jesus makes sure to point out that the father in the parable had created enough wealth in his life to provide an inheritance for his family. When relating this to our heavenly Father we see that God has given us an inheritance through the death, burial, and resurrection of Jesus.

As I shared with you earlier, my dad left me nothing as an inheritance except a small, light blue suitcase. It had a few pairs of underwear, undershirts, and a couple pairs of socks.

My dad lived a lifestyle that focused on most everything *except* his children and family. He lived for his own pleasures and desires. His focus every day was how to feed the craving of his addictions. His thoughts were continually of himself and what gratified him at that moment. There was little to no planning for the future. In other words, he was living like the wasteful son in the parable rather than like the father, who should have been his example.

It was clear that Daddy never thought enough about his kids to create some kind of wealth or foundation for us to build on. I love my daddy and in no way am I trying to make him out to be some terrible man. However, the truth is, Daddy was very selfish, and the "kingdom" he built died with him.

Jesus' focus was a lot different than Daddy's. Everything Jesus did was to save His children, provide for His children, and to create an inheritance for His people. In no way was Jesus ever self-centered.

Never do we read about Jesus fulfilling the desires of His own flesh. Everything Jesus did, said, or achieved in His life had one nucleus. That was to reestablish the Kingdom of Heaven on earth and to reunite humanity with God.

Everything was centered around the welfare of mankind and achieving the will of God.

The Word of God is clear that He, our Father, has given us an inheritance through the life of Jesus. Wealth is not an evil thing to God. God sees wealth through the eyes of a King, not the heart of a beggar.

In a kingdom, the king owns everything. In a kingdom, the attributes of the king are displayed through the quality of life he provides for his people. If the king is a good king, a loving king, and one of great character and morals, he will provide his people with good things, a loving environment, and a high quality of living.

The people of a kingdom display the attributes of the king they live under. We live under a King who is described using words such as loving, kind, faithful, just, provider, impartial, and everlasting Father. These attributes should not be used just to describe God, but if that is who He really is, then it should be displayed through lifestyle that He provides for His children.

The writers of the New Testament make it clear that the children of God are heirs to the Kingdom of Heaven and joint heirs with Jesus Himself. Jesus paid the price for His people to live a quality of life that exemplifies who God is. Yes, the Father has prepared for us an eternal inheritance, but He, through Jesus, has given us a temporal inheritance, as well. He has given us the wisdom and ability to get wealth.

His desire is that we live "*in health and prosper even as our soul does prosper.*" (3John 1:2) I could go on and on quoting scripture that proves the Father's desire for us is to live out of the inheritance Jesus provided for us.

Man has polluted the desire of God for us to live prosperous lives on earth. Prosperity is relative to a person and situation. But one thing prosperity is not is for someone to live out of the gluttony of their own ungodly pleasure.

Prosperity is living out of the inheritance Jesus purchased for us and the attributes of who our King is!

Jesus taught His disciples to pray that God's Kingdom would come *"on earth as it is Heaven."* So we should pray for Heaven to be manifested on earth. How do you think God wants to manifest Heaven on earth? I believe God wants to make Heaven real on earth through His people.

In His Word, God tells us to be anxious for nothing, to take no thought for what we should eat or drink, and not to worry about apparel and what we are to clothe ourselves with. The Bible teaches us not to concern ourselves with tomorrow for tomorrow exists in the hand of God.

Why are we commanded not to worry about these essentials? Maybe it's because we have a Father who promises to take care of those things for His children. Maybe it's because our Father has left us an inheritance to draw these essential things from.

Heaven does not exist on broken promises. Heaven does not withhold anything from its citizens. Heaven does not operate on a welfare system where its inhabitants have to beg for their King to provide them the essentials of life.

On the contrary, Heaven exists on the principles and attributes of a God that is loving, faithful, long-suffering, good, truthful, and righteous. The very foundations of Heaven are secured by who our Father is.

Jesus commanded His disciples – the first and all subsequent disciples - to pray for Earth to be run like Heaven, for our lives to manifest the nature of our Father! It can and must become a reality because *"the goodness of God draws men to repentance."* (Romans 2:4)

How can people come to know we have a good Father if we are lacking in most areas of our lives? Is there anything about a life full of heartache, poverty, sickness, and sadness that displays the goodness of God and the nature of our honest, loving King? I would say, nothing!

My Daddy left me an inheritance that displayed his nature and lifestyle. My heavenly Father has also left me an inheritance that displays His nature and lifestyle. I promise you, the inheritance our heavenly Father has left us cannot be confined to a small, light blue suitcase!

The Ability to Let Go

The next thing we see in the parable Jesus told was that the younger son came to his father and asked for his inheritance.

The Bible says, *"So he divided to them* his *livelihood."*

Upon the request of his son, the father simply gave his son what he desired. I am sure the father knew the son was not prepared to oversee such wealth. But the father had the ability and the wisdom to do something that we all need to know how to do at times, and that is to know when to just LET GO.

For years I have watched the inability to let things go destroy the lives of so many people.

It seems we would rather hold on to the hurt, pain, anger, and hatred that people have caused us than to just let it go and move on with our lives.

For many years, I held on to a lot of hurt and anger that was rooted in my heart because of the failures and decisions Daddy made - decisions that I had no control over. I couldn't go back and change Daddy's decisions, nor could I magically change the effect they had on my life. Without even realizing it, I allowed Daddy's decisions to dictate the direction of my life.

He was dead and gone and his decisions were still controlling me, all because I didn't know how to let go of his mistakes.

A lady named Shannon Alder said, "Forget what hurt you, but NEVER forget what it taught you." (I realize this woman is a believer in Mormon doctrines, but this particular statement has a lot of truth in it, nevertheless.)

I had to realize that Daddy's choices helped mold the man I am. I had to come to grips with the fact that to be the greatest me I could ever be, I had to let go of the ownership I had in the things that happened to me.

I really believe that so many people live most of their lives struggling with who they are, mostly because they are living a lie. They are living out of hurt, anger, unforgiveness, and such things. They can't find the revelation of who they are created to be, because who they are is buried underneath the people that hurt them.

Hurt will lie to you! Unforgiveness will bury you! Sinful anger will blind you from seeing your destiny! You will never know who God created you to be while holding on to the hurt others have caused you. Let them go!

75

There comes a time in every parent's life when you have to let your children go. You can't walk around with them their whole lives and instruct them on every decision they make. There comes a time you have to let them go to live and make decisions, trusting you have done your best to prepare them. They will make bad decision. They will fall short at times. They may end up spending all their wealth and dining with pigs, but you have to let them go!

If you hover over them trying to protect them, there will come a day that they resent you, because you will be the sole blame for their lack of a productive life.

Keeping a caterpillar in a cocoon does not protect it! Actually, it cripples it! Biology teaches us that a butterfly gains the strength to fly by pressing its wings up against the side walls of the cocoon. If you break open the cocoon, trying to save the poor little caterpillar, then you are actually killing the butterfly instead of saving it.

It is the same way with raising children - both spiritual and natural children. There comes a time when you have to let them go! You may see that they are walking headlong into a bad decision, but you have to let them go!

Sometimes people can only learn by the things they suffer.

The writer of Hebrews, speaking of Jesus, says, "*Although He was a Son, He learned obedience from the things which He suffered.*" (5:8)

If I were to ask you if you could go back and change certain situations in your life, would you?

Your answer would probably be "yes" to some things and "no" to others. The fact is, there are some hurts that you needed to experience. There were some failures that you needed to experience. There were some people that needed to leave you, lie to you, and misuse you! Their actions were not to destroy you, but to help create you.

There are some events that brought you pain that you would not want to go back and change. You know that those times helped secure the man or woman you are today. We, as parents or leaders, have to allow our children or those we are leading to trip and fall, not to prove they need you, but rather to prove they can get back up!

The man in the parable knew when to let go. Jesus had this ability also. The Bible teaches that, because the sun was setting and the Sabbath was approaching, the Roman soldiers had to make sure those who were crucified were dead, so they could remove them from their crosses. (John 19:31-34)

It was not lawful for bodies to be left in public on the Sabbath. This is why the soldiers were commanded to break the legs of those who were crucified. They broke their legs so they could not lift themselves up to breathe. Instead, they would suffocate, and die faster.

When they came to Jesus, however, He was already dead. Jesus knew when to fight and He knew when to let go! Jesus had to let go of life before the soldiers could break His legs because he had to fulfill all scripture. In John 19:36, the Bible says, *"For these things came to pass to fulfill the Scripture, 'NOT A BONE OF HIM SHALL BE BROKEN.'"*

Sometimes we have to let go so the prophecies and destiny over our children can be fulfilled!

This is why God designed us with our own will, our own ability to make decisions. God knew that we might not choose Him or His will for our lives. He also knew that, if we were to ever choose Him, He had to let us go to make our own decisions.

This is why He allows us to fall. Not because he enjoys seeing us in pain, but because He enjoys having the chance to pick us up and mend our wounds.

He is a GOOD Father! He is a GOOD Shepherd!

We often believe lies that say God doesn't love us and that He is not good because He allows us to make bad decisions, fall, and experience hurt. We often wonder why God could allow things to happen in our lives that cause us heartache and misfortune.

"How could you let this happen, God?"

He knows the value of letting go! We can never reach our full potential if we are not allowed to fail. We will never know God in all His glory if He does not allow us to go through some storms. He is a good Father, not because He has the ability to protect us only, but also because He has the wisdom to know when to let us go!

A Place Called Home

I have heard it said all my life that "Home is where the heart is."

That may be truer than people realize. But I am not sure you will ever know the depth of that truth until you go through a time when you don't have a home.

A good portion of my life - especially when I was very young - I knew what it was like not to have a home. My dad and mom were divorced in my first year of life. I was introduced to my third stepdad by the age of nine or ten. Because of these circumstances my sister and I were bounced around a lot for the first several years of our lives.

It's amazing what I can remember even from my earliest years: living with grandparents for a few weeks, staying at an aunt's house, or spending several nights with a friend of the family. I thank God that we had people who were willing to assist us as my family struggled through the vicissitudes of life. For a child, however, all these changes can be very damaging in many ways.

In the parable, we see a major turning point in the life of the son who spent all of his inheritance; it came when he remembered he had a home to go back to.

He remembered his father had a place prepared for him that had servants, provision, and security. In the middle of the worst time of his life, the young man's heart led him back home.

This speaks directly to the heart of our Father God. No matter how bad we mess up, He has prepared a place for our return to Him. All we have to do is remember that Jesus has paid the price for us to run into His arms at any point in our lives. The Father's love, His acceptance, His faithfulness, His security, and His strength are all attributes that describe our home where we can run to.

It's His *Presence*!

No matter what situation we find ourselves in, we have a home to return to! The prodigal son turned his whole life around once he remembered he had a place called home.

I remember growing up thinking, "One day, I will have me a single-wide trailer on some land that no one can take from me!"

My goals were not immaculate in vision because they were secured in insecurity. I longed for a place to call home so bad that I was happy with anything I could call my own. I remember praying and believing that one day I would have a trailer, an acre of land, a beautiful wife, and a son and daughter - just a place and a family that were mine. I didn't want much. I just wanted the security in knowing that it was mine and no one could take them away from me.

Well, at the age of twenty-one, I got married to my beautiful wife and we bought our single-wide trailer on an acre of land. It wasn't much, but you could not have told me it wasn't a mansion! I would go to work every day and could not wait to get home. Stephanie and I loved our little house. We were perfectly content.

We went on vacation one year and came home to find our house had been burglarized and ransacked. The only gift my Daddy ever gave me was a brass-triggered 30-30 rifle; it was stolen. Our clothes were thrown all over the house. Cabinets were opened. My wife's jewelry was gone. They even stole our tithe money we had put up until we went to church the next Sunday.

Steph and I were both so upset. She was crying and I was ready to kill whoever I could get my hands on. I don't think I was as upset about the missing items as much as I was the fact my place of security had been violated.

Our home had been mishandled by people who had no right to be there. The home I had always dreamed of and prayed for was disrespected and mistreated.

Stephanie never felt safe in that home again. She would not stay alone overnight. She would lock the doors during the day if she was alone. This was her home, but the security of that home had been murdered, probably by thug kids who had nothing better to do than steal.

They probably thought they were achieving their dreams by stealing what others had worked hard for. Not knowing that the real valuables they took with them could not fit into trash bags or be thrown over their shoulder and carried through the woods. They stole the security a family had in its home.

The young man in the parable had faith that his home was still a secure place to return to. He knew that if he could just get back home, everything would be okay. He understood that, even though he spent all his money, broken the trust of his father, and lost everything he had ever owned, if he could just get back home, everything would be made right again.

This is the foundation of our salvation and repentance!

Salvation secures a place for us to run to, a home where we can invest our hearts and know they will be protected.

The father has prepared us a place in His Presence where nothing can steal our peace. No matter how bad we mess up, He offers us a home in Him. Knowing this should make us leave the pigs and pigsty of this world and run home to Him. Nothing this world has to offer compares to the home we have in the heart of God!

Home is where the heart is, and if Jesus has our hearts, we always have a home to run to!

Your Value Comes From the Father

Luke 15:17-19 says, *"But when he came to himself, he said, 'How many of my father's hired servants have bread enough and to spare, and I perish with hunger! I will arise and go to my father, and will say to him, "Father, I have sinned against Heaven and before you, and I am no longer worthy to be called your son. Make me like one of your hired servants."""*

Here, Jesus reveals the hinge point of the son's life who had spent all of his inheritance. The turning point in the life of this young man came when he took his mind off of himself and gained his self worth from who his father was.

For a long time, the young man's life centered on his own wants and desires. He wanted his inheritance. He wanted to spend his inheritance on riotous living. He fulfilled his own lusts, not caring about the consequences his actions had on others. The young man's attitude seems to center around the thought, "Me, Me, Me!"

This is a very dangerous mindset to have! Jesus spent a lot of His earthly ministry teaching us to seek other people's well being before our own, to seek the building of His Kingdom instead of building our own. He desires for us to be very cognizant of others' wants, needs, and desires, before considering our own.

Why is this way of thinking so important to Jesus and vital to Kingdom living? I believe that one of the greatest reasons for this aligns with the principle of sowing and reaping.

Scripture says in Galatians 6:7, "*Do not be deceived, God is not mocked; for whatever a man sows, this he will also reap.*"

In other words, you cannot make a mockery of God by thinking you can sow one thing and reap something else. We get so self-centered that we often forget every decision we make will have a direct or indirect effect on others.

The young man in the parable was not thinking of how the decision to ask for and waste his inheritance would affect his dad. Nor did he consider how those decisions would affect his brother. And he certainly did not think how it would affect his own future.

All he was thinking about was self gratification, what he wanted in the moment, and how he could fulfill his own immediate desires.

He had no thought of anyone other than himself. Jesus taught that this way of thinking is not profitable and can be sinful. We will reap what we *sow*. If we sow decisions rooted in selfishness and pride, then we will reap from those seeds.

The young man in the parable changed his life the moment he changed his focal point for decision-making.

When we make decisions from a self-centered mentality, we will only reap the fruit that we can produce by ourselves. The life the young man ended up living was the best life that he could produce for himself. He ended up lonely, because loneliness is a fruit of selfishness.

He ended up broke because he sowed no seed into his future, and poverty is a fruit of self-centeredness.

The moment the young man took his focus off of himself and considered who his father was, that was the moment his life began to change for the better.

It is important for us to live our lives centered around who our heavenly Father is and not on who we are.

It is who the Father is that brings value to us. This is why God gave us the name of Jesus. The name that is above every other name!

Philippians 2:9 states, "*Wherefore also God highly exalted him, and gave unto him the name which is above every name*." God gave Jesus a name higher and more powerful than any other name, and Jesus, in turn, gave us His name to live and operate under. So we are victorious, not by our own name or efforts, but by who Jesus is and the victory He has won.

The first thing the enemy wants you to do in battle is to evaluate yourself and what you can do in your own power. That is what King David's brothers and Goliath tried to do to him. They tried to put the focus on David and his weaknesses. They made comments that questioned his abilities, his appearance, his preparation for battle, his stature, his intentions, and the like.

The great thing about King David is, he already knew and was comfortable with his own inadequacies. King David had already learned that his victory didn't depend on him or his abilities. Rather, the victory David was seeking would be won because of who his Daddy was!

When Goliath and others tried to emphasize David's weaknesses, it did not deter him in the least. Why? Because David knew his strength was found in who his God was.

David valued himself by who his heavenly Father was, and not who he was, alone.

We also see this principle taught all through the life of Jesus. He was constantly pointing to the Father when asked to prove who He, himself, was. He said things like, "*If you have seen me you have seen the Father*," and "*I only do the things I see the Father do.*"

What we have to learn from Jesus' comments is that He knew His self worth came from God His Father.

Jesus' ability to live in victory derived from His ability to focus on who His Father was. Everything Jesus did or said pointed back to His Father.

For years I struggled with my own self worth because of who my earthly father was. I limited myself and my future by who my daddy was, and the mistakes he made. However, the moment I realized that my value comes from who my eternal, heavenly Father is – that was the moment I was able to escape my own pig pin.

What I want to tell you with all the emotion and passion within me is, YOUR VALUE COMES FROM YOUR FATHER!

You are strong, victorious, wise, competent, and secure in being successful because these things describe who your heavenly Father is. He is all wisdom, He is all powerful, He is everlasting, He is almighty, He is the same yesterday today and forever - this is who your Father is!

In turn, this is who you are! You have been given HIS NAME! His name accompanies every attribute His nature displays. When the Bible says He has given us His name, to abide under it is meaning, we have been given His full authority.

In one sense, I loved growing up in Duluth, Georgia, with the last name Edmondson. The Edmondsons were known to be generous, successful, caring, and strong fighters that you didn't want to mess with. I held my head up and was prideful because of the Edmondson name.

However, the older I got, and the more mistakes my daddy made, the view of the name I was carrying changed. The way I saw myself changed. The value I found in myself changed, because the value my dad placed on my life decreased.

On the other hand, the way I valued myself changed very rapidly for the better when I found out who my real Father was and is.

Unharness your potential by drawing your value from your Father!

Colossians 2:9-10 tells us, "*For in Him dwells all the fullness of the Godhead bodily; and <u>you are complete in Him</u>, who is the head of all principality and power.*"

The Prodigal Father

As I stated in the chapter summary earlier, the topic of this parable in Luke 15 changed in my mind once Holy Spirit showed me the point was not about the sons but about the father.

I want you to read again Luke 15:18-24:

"*I will arise and go to my father, and will say unto him, Father, I have sinned against Heaven, and before thee, and am no more worthy to be called thy son: make me as one of*

86

thy hired servants. And he arose, and came to his father. <u>But when he was yet a great way off, his father saw him, and had compassion, and ran, and fell on his neck, and kissed him.</u> And the son said unto him, Father, I have sinned against Heaven, and in thy sight, and am no more worthy to be called thy son. But the father said to his servants, Bring forth the best robe, and put it on him; and put a ring on his hand, and shoes on his feet: And bring hither the fatted calf, and kill it; and let us eat, and be merry: For this my son was dead, and is alive again; he was lost, and is found. And they began to be merry."

WOW! I love this parable so much! We must understand that when Jesus told parables, oftentimes He would hide within the parable the nature and attributes of God the Father. The underlined sentence above shows what kind of Father we have. He loves us so much!

The Scripture says, "But when he was a great way off the father saw him…" The son never even made it back home before the father responded to his return!

What does that say about our God? It says that He is waiting on us to run to Him! The wording here provides us with the thought that the father was in constant attention, longing for the son to return. We don't have to convince our Father to love us and to forgive us. He is anxiously waiting for us to come to Him so He can lavish His nature on us!

The word "prodigal" means to have or give something on a lavishing scale. It means to be extravagant, reckless, prodigious or even wasteful. Those adjectives can seem bad, but when describing the Father's love and mercy towards His children, they are amazing!

Our Father is a "Prodigal Father"!

He recklessly loves us! He is extravagant in displaying His heart towards His children! He pours out Himself on us to the point it seems wasteful!

This is what the father in Jesus' parable did, and it reveals how our Father God responds toward us. This is the way prodigal fathers always respond. Prodigal fathers respond through reckless abandonment of their own wants, needs, or desires to meet the needs of their children.

Jesus is the perfect example of a prodigal father. He left everything to take on the weight of the sin of man. He left Heaven's glory and splendor to put on the garments of heaviness and rejection. He did it all for us!

Why?

Because he is a prodigal Father, a Father that is reckless, extravagant, and even "wasteful" concerning loving, forgiving, and chasing after His children.

I grew up with little contact with my dad. So I was taught that, if I wanted time with Daddy or wanted him to be pleased with me, I had to pursue him. I had to be the one that chased after Daddy.

On the other hand, if I made a bad decision or messed up, Daddy would withdraw from me in anger and disappointment. So I had that perception of God. I thought my heavenly Father responded to my failure and inadequacies the same way my natural parents did. However, after being in relationship with the Lord for many years, I found it is not in His nature to reject his children. He doesn't draw away from us when we fail. In fact, scripture teaches that it's our imperfections that draw Him to us. Paul taught that while we were yet sinners, Christ died for us. (Romans 5:8)

The first reaction we see from the father in the parable is compassion. A prodigal father always reacts out of prodigious compassion for his children. If you're a pastor, teacher, evangelist, apostle, prophet, or church leader, the best thing you can do for those following you is to be a prodigal father or mother in their lives.

If you're a parent, choose to parent from the position of prodigious love, one who responds with compassion first. See your children, or those you are leading, from far off and run to meet them with compassion. Do like the man in the parable and run as fast as you can to them and wrap them in your arms, kiss their necks, and love them prodigiously!

I am convinced that if the five-fold ministry is to operate in the fullness that God intended, then we must drop our titles and simply embrace being prodigal leaders.

We have to be leaders who demonstrate selfless love for those God has entrusted to us. You will never be an effective leader if you react to people the way they react to you and/or each other. You must be spiritually and emotionally mature. That's why you are a LEADER! To be different. To respond differently. To live differently.

We, as ministers of the Gospel, are created to carry the image of the Father. God does not react to His children in haste, anger, unforgiveness, resentment, or anything like this. We sometimes feel like we have a right to be mean, disrespectful, or harsh, or correct with a strong arm. However, it is never okay to falsely portray the nature of the Father to those you are leading.

If you are angry at someone, postpone meeting with them. If your emotions are raw concerning a topic, then don't address it until you can address it with love. Be wise and give no place to the devil!

Just because God has called you, and man has appointed you, doesn't mean you're released from treating God's people the way He would. Decide in your heart that you will be a prodigal leader. Determine today that you will be a prodigal parent. Go in to work tomorrow and do business as a prodigal employer.

Display the character of the One who saw you coming afar off and ran to you with loving care, the One who wrapped you in arms of love and acceptance, the One who kisses you with the kisses of compassion.

Choose to be a natural example of the spiritual Prodigal Father!

For years, I longed to be embraced in the arms of a loving father. To rest in the embrace of a father that had nothing motivating him other than his desire to hold me.

I never received this love from my natural daddy. My outstretched arms were often knocked away by his persistent absence. A heart that was opened to loving correction, that searched for strength and wisdom, was too often slammed shut by the rejection of broken promises.

I was living wounded. I made decisions from a place of pain and heartache. I was living out the saying, "Hurting people hurt people." I did not set out to hurt people, but you can only produce from the seeds that dominate the garden of your emotions. The seeds planted in my emotional makeup were producing a crop of recycled rejection, separation, guilt, and self-hatred.

That was, until I met my Prodigal Father!

He has taught me what real love is. He has shown me how a real Father reacts to my failures. He has, and continues to, run to me with open arms and committed kisses. All you have to do is the same thing I did: release all the emotions that reign in your life through the inabilities of your natural parents, friends, and other relational influences, and let Holy Spirit embrace you as the Prodigal Father that He is!

He is looking for you! He is anticipating your arrival! Just as the man in the parable reacted to his son, the Father is sure to respond to you.

People need arms to fall into.

You do, I do, the young man in the parable did, and those you are parenting and/or leading do.

The question is, will you provide those arms? Will you become the prodigal person they need? If your answer is yes, then you must first allow the prodigal embrace that is reaching out to you.

Forgiveness... An Attribute of the Father

Another amazing truth about this story is the fact that Jesus never speaks of the father forgiving the son.

He didn't demand the son go through a restoration process. We don't read that the man ever told the son he forgave him. I don't think Jesus thought it needed to be addressed because, with God, forgiveness is just His nature. It is not something the Father has to be convinced to do.

The Church has made repentance and forgiveness hard. But with God, this process is so simple. Repentance and forgiveness are really one thing to God. You cannot separate the two because God views repentance and forgiveness as the same thing. It is like light and darkness.

How can that be?

The Psalmist said in Psalms 139:12 that "...*darkness and light are the same to you* (God)." Darkness does not exist in God's Presence. The moment we repent, forgiveness is available. There is no space or time between the two. There is no process of restoration. God just begins to kill the fatted calf and initiate and celebrate His child that has come home.

We hide resentment and unforgiveness behind statements like, "Well I forgive, but I don't forget."

Do you know that saying is not backed by scripture, nor is it found in the nature of God. Scripture teaches, and God's nature is revealed in, the power to forget and forgive the sins of others. We know that the moment we repent, God forgives us and, at the same time, casts the memory of our failure into the sea of forgetfulness.

Or as scripture says in Psalms103:12 *"As far as the east is from the west, so far hath he removed our transgressions from us."*

So, when we say we have the ability to forgive, but do not forget, we are lying. Forgiving and forgetting are one and the same, just like repentance and forgiving. They walk hand in hand. Forgiveness is an attribute of prodigal people.

When someone truly repents to you, your only response is to forgive them and forget the trespass forever. When you choose to hold on to the memory of what they did to you, you are forever tying yourself to the pain of the event. Let it go!

The man in the parable didn't have to be convinced to forgive his son. It was his natural response. It seemed to be an easy choice, because his longing to have his son back home trumped his need to get even or to have his feelings validated.

It's the same way with God. He is waiting and longing for us to reconcile with Him. His forgiveness is quick and thorough. His memory is cleansed by our repentance. He offers a fresh start at the hint of repentance. No coercion needed.

It is His nature.

Chapter 5

Who's Your Daddy?

The Father of Reconciliation

The son who went out and spoiled his inheritance on riotous living had one desire from his father.

In verse 21 of Luke 15, the son said to his father, *"Father, I have sinned against Heaven, and in thy sight, and <u>am no more worthy to be called thy son</u>."*

The only thing the son asked of the father was that he would forgive him and allow him to be a servant within his father's kingdom. This is the way we approach God a lot of times.

We know that we have made a mess of our lives. We get that we may have handled a situation in the wrong way. We make God promises and then break them or fail to stay committed to them. So, once we allow God to convince us to come to Him, we come with a servant's mentality. Our thought is, Lord I am not worthy to be called a son or daughter any longer. So we settle for the thought of being a servant in the Kingdom.

Well, Jesus did not die for you to be a servant in His Kingdom. He died for you to be reconciled back to Him as His child!

The Father is a Father of reconciliation! Look at how the man in the story reacted to his son's request to be a servant. The man immediately restored his son to the place of sonship. He killed the fatted calf *for* him.

He replaced the robe the son had lost with a better robe. He replaced the ring the son had lost with a new ring. He put new shoes on his feet. He called for a celebration because his son came home. The man restored his son's sonship and authority!

It is human nature to require payment for failure. It takes time to restore trust, but God is so powerful that he removes time from the equation when forgiving and reconciling His children. That's an attribute of a prodigal father. Prodigal fathers forgive and reconcile their children immediately.

The son lost his robe and would have been satisfied with a servant's robe, but the father gave him "the best" robe. The son squandered his wealth and traded his signet ring. He would have been happy with no ring as long as he had a place to live. However, that is not the nature of a prodigal father.

The father gave his repentant son a place to live, a new ring, new shoes, and he restored his old position within the kingdom. This is the way God reconciles with us! He doesn't set us back on a lower rung of the ladder. He restores us as sons and daughters, with the best robe, a new ring, new shoes, and He throws a party for our return.

I love the quote that says, "The enemy knows your name, but calls you by your faults. God knows your faults, but calls you by your name." I am not sure where it originated, but it is packed full of truth.

The enemy hates to think that we are children of God. He doesn't want you to know how valuable you are to the

Father, and how much the Father longs to love and care for you. All he wants you to do is continue to identify yourself by your mistakes. But you are not what you have done!

One of the worst things you can do when coming into the presence of God is to come in identifying yourself by your past. It may be, if we come to the Father with this mindset, that he doesn't recognize us, because He has forgotten our past. I know it sounds peculiar and a little weird, but the point may be valid.

After Adam and Eve chose to believe the enemy and sin against God, He didn't recognize them.

Genesis 3:8-9 says, "*They* (Adam and Eve) *heard the sound of the LORD God walking in the garden in the cool of the day, and the man and his wife hid themselves from the presence of the LORD God among the trees of the garden. Then the LORD God called to the man, and said to him, 'Where are you?'*"

Jewish theology teaches that, because God is omnipresent and omnipotent, this scripture could not mean that God did not know where to locate Adam and Eve, but rather, that there was confusion about the state of being they were living in. However, we know God was not confused. He knew exactly where they were and the dire consequences brought about by their sin. The scripture is trying to show that God did not know them in their changed condition, or that God no longer "recognized" them, and His question was only rhetorical.

I think, along the same lines, when we come to God beaten down and servant-minded, we are confined by our past mistakes. It brings confusion to our communication with the Father. He is waiting on His son or daughter, and we show up as wounded servants and sinners.

When we come to the Father we must be Kingdom-minded. We come to Him as the redeemed, saved, restored, reconciled children that we are!

The young man was happy just to be in the kingdom. He was satisfied being a servant. However, the father was not going to allow his child to be a servant. It was not up for debate. The father did what was in his heart to do because he was a prodigal father.

The young man's state of mind did not change the reaction of the father. The young man seemingly forgot that his worth came from who his father was, not from his failures. Don't ever believe the lie of the enemy that tells you that you are what you have done. You are not your mistakes! Your value comes from who your Daddy is!

Jesus has reconciled us to the Father. We have been justified by His grace, love, and mercy, just as if we had never sinned or failed! Stop settling for being a servant. God has qualified you to be His child. Servants have no inheritance. Scripture teaches us that we have the same inheritance as Jesus.

God calls us His children every time! Every time! Not because of who we are, what we have done or will do. He calls us children because of who He is. He is the Father of reconciliation. He loves to restore us. He loves to pick us up and show us off. He looks upon us and says - like my Dad said the time I walked into the cancer hospice -"That's my boy!"

You are His! Your value will never change because He will never change. Hebrews 13:8 says, *"Jesus Christ is the same yesterday and today and forever."*

If you were worthy enough to receive the love and grace of God while you were His "enemy," then how much more worthy are you now that you are His child? *"For if while we were enemies we were reconciled to God through the death of His Son, much more, having been reconciled, we shall be saved by His life."* (Romans 5:10 NASV)

Don't "serve" Him: be like Him.

After all, He is your Daddy!

Who Is This Masked Man?

Many times in my life, I carried resentment towards my dad simply because of the things I heard about him.

I was not able to spend a whole lot of time with him, so I only knew him by the stories I was told. The problem with that was, most of the stories I was told were coming from a bitter mother, a heart-broken sister, or wounded family members.

Their stories and evaluation of who my daddy was were tainted with their own unresolved issues. So, for many years, I grew up loving - and even at times, hating - a man I didn't really know. My emotions were tied to the stories I had heard. When the stories aligned with Daddy's actions, then I felt every story was validated. I believed every judgment placed on Daddy by most people. His failures to show up when promised seemed to root the desperate emotions even deeper into my heart.

Later in life, I spent more time with Daddy and I got to see for myself that all the stories did not accurately describe who he really was. Sure, he had plenty of flaws, but he was a wounded man, himself.

It took many years for me to see who my dad really was because, for years, I was in relationship with a man whose real heart had been masked. Once I had a personal relationship with the man, the mask came off and I was able to judge the person he was for myself.

I feel like this is the relationship most Christian people have with the Lord. They only know Him from the stories they have read or heard. They have heard how God is good, He is love, He is faithful, and He is just. But because they have little to no relationship with Him, when He doesn't show up the way He has been described, they build up resentment and anger towards Him.

It is a dangerous thing to have opinions about someone based on what you have heard about them. Hearing stories about someone does not warrant reaction towards that person. It is not fair to harbor ill will toward someone based on what you have heard about them. Stories, emotions, and feelings can often mask the real person.

Many Christians are in a relationship with a masked Man whose character they do not know. I thank God for the stories about Jesus. I love to hear what God has done in the lives of others. I love to hear about His miracles. My faith is stirred when people share with me the things Holy Spirit reveals to them. However, my opinion of who God is does not come from any story shared.

My view of His character comes from the relationship that I have with Him. This is very important. So when the stories, reports or revelations do not line up with who I know He is, I don't receive them as truth. I was not able to draw this line when hearing stories about Daddy, because I didn't have a relationship with him that proved otherwise.

I am afraid the Church today is in love with a masked Man, a partial image of a Father that is tainted with others' broken dreams and broken hearts. Many don't have a strong enough personal relationship with the Father to dispute the stories that they hear about Him.

They believe whatever anyone says, so when they try to come to the Father, intimacy is not achieved because the face they are looking into does not resemble the face that been described to them. His personality, His heart, His ways, His plans stay concealed behind the mask of other peoples' evaluations.

I love the scripture reference, 1John 3:1-3:
"See how great a love the Father has bestowed on us, that we would be called children of God; and such we are. For this reason the world does not know us, because it did not know Him. Beloved, now we are children of God, and it has not appeared as yet what we will be. We know that when He appears, we will be like Him, because we will see Him just as He is. And everyone who has this hope fixed on Him purifies himself, just as He is pure."

John's conviction was that we don't know what or who we are because it has not been shown to us in complete purity and honesty.

He says that the moment we see God just as He is, we can be like Him. Not as a masked man. Not a man hidden behind the stories of others, nor confined to the revelations of others. But when He appears, we will be like Him - no process, no instruction classes, and no makeover. We will become like

Him, simply because the mask will be taken away and we will really see Him JUST AS HE IS.

Daddy was not this terrible, vindictive, destructive, abusive man that had been described to me. The stories were not completely true about his character. Sometimes the facts of the stories were accurate, but the intent from which the facts arose did not reveal the true nature of the person that did the acts.

This is important to remember when you read about God in the Bible, especially in the Old Testament. When you read that He sent fire and brimstone down upon Sodom and Gomorrah, you have to know His character to understand why He reacted the way He did. Likewise, to understand why God would ask Abraham to offer his only son, Isaac, as a burnt offering to Him, only comes when you know God's true intent and motive.

You can't just read or hear stories about what God did or did not do and then draw an accurate description of who He is. You must KNOW Him!

Read and hear the cry of Paul's heart shared in Philippians 3:1-11:
"Finally, my brethren, rejoice in the Lord. To write the same things again is no trouble to me, and it is a safeguard for you. Beware of the dogs, beware of the evil workers, beware of the false circumcision; for we are the true circumcision, who worship in the Spirit of God and glory in Christ Jesus and put no confidence in the flesh, although I myself might have confidence even in the flesh. If anyone else has a mind to put confidence in the flesh, I far more: circumcised the eighth day, of the nation of Israel, of the tribe of Benjamin, a Hebrew of Hebrews; as to the Law, a Pharisee; as to zeal, a persecutor of the church; as to the righteousness which is in

the Law, found blameless. But whatever things were gain to me, those things I have counted as loss for the sake of Christ. More than that, I count all things to be loss in view of the surpassing value of knowing Christ Jesus my Lord, for whom I have suffered the loss of all things, and count them but rubbish so that I may gain Christ, and may be found in Him, not having a righteousness of my own derived from the Law, but that which is through faith in Christ, the righteousness which comes from God on the basis of faith, that I may know Him and the power of His resurrection and the fellowship of His sufferings, being conformed to His death; in order that I may attain to the resurrection from the dead."

Paul's heart expression was to KNOW God. He didn't want his relationship with God to be masked by religious ceremonies, doctrines, natural bloodlines, or reports from ungodly people. His desire was to know God in whatever revealed His true identity and character. He wanted to know God's victorious power, His enduring faithfulness, and His dying commitment to His people.

It was these characteristics and His noble, loving character that revealed God's true nature.

Paul was saying, If I have to be crucified and resurrected again to know Him, then put the nails in my hands. He was crying out that, if he had to suffer the sufferings of Christ in order to have intimate knowledge of God's character, then bring on the sufferings.

Paul was even willing to die if that's what it took to KNOW God in all His splendor and glory. He longed to witness the Father without any mask on His face. He wasn't satisfied with just hearing the stories about Him. The mere image of God was no longer satisfying to Paul. He wanted to embrace the Person of God Himself, no matter the cost! Paul was crying out, in effect, "Unmask my Father and let me see Him!"

My desire for you in writing this chapter is that you will no longer be satisfied with having a relationship with a God that wears a mask, one that you might have put on him by simply hearing Him described by others.

Take the mask off of Him and see Him for who He is!

That is what God desires for you to do.

I understand that He may not have appeared to be the way you wanted Him to at times, but allow Him to reveal His true identity to you and His motives will be evident as you see His true face.

God had to make some serious decisions concerning the children of Israel. Regardless, we never see Moses lose faith in who God was.

Why? Maybe it's because Moses was constantly in God's face, so to speak.

Exodus 33:11 says, *"Thus the LORD used to speak to Moses face to face, just as a man speaks to his friend."*

Moses was not swayed by the acts of God because he knew the nature of God. He trusted the character of the unmasked Man he saw while in His Presence.

God's acts were justified by His character. When Moses couldn't trace God's hand, he knew he could trust His Heart! You, too, can trust God's heart!

Remove the mask from His face, so He can reveal to you who He really is, and, in turn, you will know who you really are!

Maybe you have that feeling of being lost or incomplete because you are being directed by a masked Man, a veiled God, a tainted image.

He doesn't want to be hidden behind the stories you have been told about him any longer. He wants you to reach up and pull the mask off of Him, and look into His face.

In doing so, you will no longer have to ask the question, "Who is that masked Man?"

Trusting Someone Who Has Always Failed You

One of the hardest things I had to overcome once Jesus Christ became my Lord and Savior, and my Father, was the ability to trust Him.

How do you trust someone who has always failed you? This was the question I had to have answered. Not that God had ever failed me, but the only father I had ever known failed me so often that I felt I couldn't trust *any* father figure.

Trust means having firm confidence in the reliability, truth, ability, or strength of someone or something. Trust requires you to be vulnerable, and to put your life, your emotions, and the outcome of your future into someone else's hands.

When speaking of a father, every one I had trusted failed me miserably. When I came into covenant with a God that wants to relate to me as Father to son, I was scared. It took me a long time to be able to trust the Lord to do what He said He would do.

Trust is not something that forms quickly; it will not be completed over a weekend. Trust comes over time, only when someone is given the opportunity to fail, leave, forget, break covenant, or lie to you, but, instead, remains true. It comes when such a person's love for you, and the desire to be everything you need him or her to be, drives that one to be in and keep covenant with you.

It's in these kinds of circumstances that trust is conceived and birthed.

It takes time to really build trust in a relationship. If your trust has been molested and misused, then it takes even longer for trust to be rebirthed within your heart.

But our Prodigal Father is a patient Father. He allows us to question His faithfulness as He builds the trust between us. He is not like men; He doesn't run when questioned.

People get fickle and high-minded when their motives are questioned. If you want to see someone's real motives, question his or her heart.

God does not mind our questions because His motives are pure. Everything He does, He does with His children in mind. If for no other reason, we can trust God because of what Hebrews 4:15 tells us. It says, *"For we do not have a high priest who cannot sympathize with our weaknesses, but One who has been tempted in all things as we are, yet without sin."*

We can trust God and embrace Him as our Father because He knows what it is like to be us.

105

There is nothing you will face that Jesus did not walk through in some perspective.

He was rejected by those He loved most. He heard the murmurings around town about his conception. There is no telling the comments Jesus heard about His mother and her virgin conception! Maybe the kids made fun of Him because no one really knew who His daddy was. It is easier for us to receive Jesus' virgin birth because we are not living in that time. We have heard the story all our lives.

Imagine, however, if the young lady next door who is engaged to the construction worker down the road ended up pregnant. Would you believe her if she sat down with you and told you her baby was conceived in virginity? Do you think anyone would believe her if she said that she and the construction worker had never had sex? What about when the child began to attend school, and when the daddy that came to the PTA meeting looked nothing like the child? Would they have any credibility with the kids and faculty at school?

"Oh yeah!" people would say. "It's because the kid's conception was miraculous!" How do you think the kids would treat the "miracle" child?

I am sure Jesus heard the rumors. He experienced the rejection. Not everyone wanted the miracle child playing with their precious children. Jesus was a little weird to the people of His time. Other kids were out being kids and Jesus was memorizing scripture and spending time with priests and scholars.

We can trust Jesus with our lives because He can relate to our pain.

I began to trust God when I realized that Jesus longed to be embraced by His absent Father just like I did. My trust in God grew when I learned that even His Father left Him when He needed Him the most, on the cross. That's where Jesus proclaimed to His Father, "*My God, My God, why have you forsaken me?*"

He reached out to a Father that could not, at that moment, embrace Him back. God the Father had to withhold His embrace from Jesus so that He would not have to withhold His embrace from us!

You can trust Jesus because He knows what it is like to be you! You can't trust someone with your heart who can't relate to your pain. This is why the marriage commitment is through sickness and in health, for better or worse, throughout good times and bad.

Why do we confine our marriage union with these parameters? Because marriage is all about being able to trust each other.

Trust is built on the battlefields, not on the mountaintops, when you go through struggles together and stay loyal. Marriage is based in the ability to fight through the battles of life, without turning your weapons on one another. It's these battles that create a common ground and common bond between the married couple. Because the couple can relate to each other's temptations, they can trust each other with their lives.

The Bible constantly draws a comparison between marriage and our relationship with God. Analogies use words like bride, bridegroom, wedding, wedding feast, husband, and so on.

In Ephesians 5:32, Paul makes that comparison in his instructions to husbands for their wives: *"This mystery is great; but I am speaking with reference to Christ and the church."*

Why does Paul compare our relationship with God to a marriage? Because it teaches us that no matter what we go through, God will never break our trust! He is committed to us all the time, in every way, through every situation.

You can trust him!

It took me a while to realize I could trust God, His Word, and His investment into my future, even while His Word declares Him to be faithful.

He is the same yesterday, today, and forever. (Hebrews 13:8)

He will never leave me nor forsake me. (Deuteronomy 31:8)

His ways are not my ways, but His way is always the right way.

He is faithful and He is true.

I could go on and on about who the Father has proven to be, but none of that will do any good if you don't learn to release Him from the whipping post you have erected for Him because of the pain others have caused you.

Trusting my daddy was not an option for me. He proved time and time again that he could not be trusted. He proved the investment of my trust placed in him would yield an increase of frustration, pain, heartache, and confusion.

But God has proven to me that placing my trust in Him always yields a great harvest of love, acceptance, security, and wholeness.

How can you trust someone who has always failed you? You can't. However, you can replace the one who has always failed you with one who has never, will never, and can never fail you! He is your heavenly Father. He is trustworthy. He is passionate about you.

His caring plans for you are affirmed in Jeremiah 29:11, where God says, *"For I know the thoughts that I think toward you, saith the LORD, thoughts of peace, and not of evil, to give you an expected end."*

You may not have anyone else in your life that you can trust, but you can trust Him!

He is the Prodigal Father, the one that sees you coming to Him afar off and He comes running to meet you with arms outstretched, and with prodigious love and grace.

He will not reject you. He will not misuse your trust. He is your Father full of faith and love. His arms are strong, His commitment is everlasting, and His promises to you are eternal.

The Posthumous Father

I want to share an amazing scripture with you.

Romans 5:1-9 says,
"Therefore, having been justified by faith, we have peace with God through our Lord Jesus Christ, through whom also we have obtained our introduction by faith into this grace in

which we stand; and we exult in hope of the glory of God. And not only this, but we also exult in our tribulations, knowing that tribulation brings about perseverance; and perseverance, proven character; and proven character, hope; and hope does not disappoint, because the love of God has been poured out within our hearts through the Holy Spirit who was given to us. For while we were still helpless, at the right time Christ died for the ungodly. For one will hardly die for a righteous man; though perhaps for the good man someone would dare even to die. <u>But God demonstrates His own love toward us, in that while we were yet sinners, Christ died for us.</u> Much more then, having now been justified by His blood, we shall be saved from the wrath of God through Him."

I want to single out verse 8, where it says, "*But God demonstrates His own love toward us, in that while we were yet sinners, Christ died for us.*"

The writer lets us in on an incredible concept of who Jesus is and our relationship with Him. We see that, while we were dead in our sins, and before we were even born into this world, Christ died for us. So our Father, Jesus, died for us before we were ever born spiritually and physically.

That makes God a Posthumous Father.

A "Posthumous father" is a father who has died before his children were born, meaning that he impregnated a woman, and, for whatever reason, died before the child could be birthed. This is the type of Father that our God is. Before we were born again, when we were dead to Him in our sin, He died for us!

Some 2000 years before we were even born, Jesus had already died for us. The promised seed of our destiny had been spoken into time, but our Father died before our time of birth. The work of the Father was completed while we were dead, not yet born again from our sinful state. The importance of knowing that is so we can understand that nothing beyond our salvation is required of us to be His children! There is nothing we can do to stay His children. He did the work before we were even born!

According to legal documentation, posthumous birth has special implications in law, potentially affecting a child's citizenship and legal rights, inheritances, and order of succession. Legal systems generally include special provisions regarding inheritance by posthumous children and the legal status of such children.

Law states that a posthumous child is treated as having been living at the death of the parent, meaning that the child receives the same share of the parent's estate as if the child had been born before the parent's death. Let me break this down for you.

Citizenship: Children who had posthumous births receive the citizenship of their father even though he died prior to their birth. What does that mean to you and me? It means that, because our Father was not a citizen of this world or limited to its laws and restrictions, then we are not citizens of this world either!

The Bible says it like this, in Ephesians 2:19:
"So then you are no longer strangers and aliens, but you are fellow citizens with the saints, and are of God's household."

Also, Philippians 3:20 says, *"For our citizenship is in Heaven, from which also we eagerly wait for a Savior, the Lord Jesus Christ."*

2 Corinthians 5:20 says, *"Therefore, we are ambassadors for Christ, as though God were making an appeal through us; we beg you on behalf of Christ, be reconciled to God."*

The definition of an ambassador is "an accredited diplomat sent as its official representative to a foreign country."

Paul describes us as people who are not citizens of this world, but as being sent to this world to establish the rights and benefits of the country of our citizenship. You are an ambassador of Heaven! You are here to establish the laws of your Father's country. Your assignment is to live as an example of the country of your citizenship.

An area will eventually take on the attributes of the dominant culture in it. In the 1800s and early 1900s, when countries conquered other countries, they would infiltrate the new area with their citizens. They would require the native people to speak their language, follow their customs, and obey their laws.

Before long, many characteristics of the native people groups disappeared, having been conformed to the newcomer culture. People dressed the same, spoke the same, and had the same mannerisms. Their lifestyles would change so much that their priorities would change, as well. It happened because their land was strategically infiltrated by the leaders and citizens of the conquering country.

This is what Jesus did. He came and brought His Kingdom with Him. He reestablished His Kingdom on earth and gave us the mandate to occupy, or rule it until he comes back.

This is why Paul told the Church of Rome, *"And do not be conformed to this world, but be transformed by the renewing of your mind, so that you may prove what the will of God is, that which is good and acceptable and perfect."* (Romans 12:2)

We are not to conform to the language, customs, rituals, and mannerisms of this world. Our Father gave us His citizenship and wants us to establish His values in this world.

Natural and legal rights According to Wikipedia, "Natural and legal rights are two types of rights. Natural rights are those that are not dependent on the laws or customs of any particular culture or government, and so are universal and inalienable. They cannot be repealed by human laws, though one can forfeit their enforcement through one's actions, such as by violating someone else's rights. Legal rights are those bestowed onto a person by a given legal system. They can be modified, repealed, and restrained by human laws."[1]

There are certain rights you have as a child of God, rights that invoke obedience to spiritual law. For instance, once you are born again, you are not under the law of sin and death.

Romans 8:1-4 says,
"Therefore there is now no condemnation for those who are in Christ Jesus. <u>For the law of the Spirit of life in Christ Jesus has set you free from the law of sin and of death</u>. For what the Law could not do, weak as it was through the flesh, God did: sending His own Son in the likeness of sinful flesh and as an offering for sin, He condemned sin in the flesh, so that the requirement of the Law might be fulfilled in us, who do not walk according to the flesh but according to the Spirit."

We are not a lawless people, for the law of the Spirit has replaced the law of sin and death as the ruling force over

---

[1] https://en.wikipedia.org/wiki/Natural_and_legal_rights

God's children. As an American, I understand that I am free, not because my country is lawless, but rather because it has its own system of laws in force.

We live in a Christian generation that teaches we can live and act any way we want to, because we are not under the law. But the truth is, we are under a system of enforced laws. But it is the system of laws our Father God enforces. That is a major reason God has sent Holy Spirit, for He will lead and guide us into all truth. (John 16:13)

It's important for us to know that we are under spiritual law, so we can revolt against any natural or legal law that is contrary to our law and seeks to be enforced upon us. When I say "revolt against," I am not necessarily speaking of natural hostility. I am speaking about revolting or fighting in the spirit.

For instance, if sickness or disease attacks your body, you can choose to receive the sickness to control your body. Or you can tap into the law of your Father, and not receive that sickness into your body.

Isaiah said, when prophesying about Jesus, "*But he was wounded for our transgressions, he was bruised for our iniquities: the chastisement of our peace was upon him; and with his stripes we are healed.*"

Jesus fulfilled the requirement of spiritual law for four main things stated in this prophecy: forgiveness of our sin, wiping away our immorality, restoring our peace, healing for our fleshly bodies. Our Posthumous Father has fulfilled the natural and legal laws that were against us, and has imputed to us another law that governs our lives for His glory.

I carry my natural daddy's name. My name is John David Edmondson, Jr. My dad's name was the exact same, minus the Jr. Up until my daddy died, I had to make sure I signed any legal document with the suffix, Jr. If I didn't, they would mistake me for my dad and, in certain situations, I could get into a lot of trouble.

For instance, when my wife and I first got married and applied for a loan to purchase our home, I had to use the suffix, Jr., with my name. The reason was, my dad had no credit. He paid cash for everything, and had never had a loan or bill in his name. We would have been turned down for the loan if I had used my dad's name for the credit check.

If I were to fill out a request to visit an inmate in jail or prison, I had to be sure and use the suffix, Jr. If not, they would mistake me for my dad, and there would be no way I could go into the jail or prison, because of his record.

Why is this important to you? Because I want to show you the legal effect the name you carry will have on your situations. The Bible teaches, and I alluded to previously, that God gave Jesus a name that is above every other name, that at the name of Jesus, every knee should bow, both in this world and the world to come.

We, as His children, carry His name! His name carries supreme authority for the enforcement of spiritual law! Natural law has to bow to the name of our Father. Spiritual legal systems against us (powers and principalities of darkness) must surrender their power to us as God's children the moment we use His name against them!

There are spiritual laws that govern humanity, laws that we must obey if we want to reap the benefits of such laws. Sowing and reaping, seed time and harvest, the law of dominion, the law of confession, the law of first mention, are just a few of those laws.

If we know, understand, and obey the law of sowing and reaping, we can reap the benefits of obeying that law. Whatsoever you sow, of that you will also reap.

When you know, understand, and implement the law of dominion, you use your dominion as a child of God to govern the affairs of your life. Nothing can enforce dominion over you when you are subject to God's law of dominion.

I could go on and on, but I just want to show that you have a Posthumous Father that died before you were born, or born again (saved), and He left you a system of law to be in force over your life.

Inheritance: I think it is so important to know and understand that we, as children of God, have basically two realms of inheritance.

One realm is the inheritance we will receive in eternity. It exists in eternity, and is the inheritance concerning God's promises to us that we will receive and enjoy in the New Heaven and New Earth. John speaks of this inheritance in Revelation. I am not going to take time to explain this inheritance to you, but we will receive things such as eternal life, gowns of salvation, robes of righteousness, freedom from tears of sorrow, and white stones (of innocence) with a new name on it for each of us.

Here, I really want to focus on the second realm of inheritance, which is the realm of inheritance most people don't even know about. This realm of inheritance is the realm of life that we are living in now.

Jesus didn't die for our eternal inheritance alone, but He also died to reestablish our dominion and inheritance in this present time and world.

Ephesians 1:6-14 says,
"To the praise of the glory of his grace, wherein he hath made us accepted in the beloved. In whom we have redemption through his blood, the forgiveness of sins, according to the riches of his grace; Wherein he hath abounded toward us in all wisdom and prudence; Having made known unto us the mystery of his will, according to his good pleasure which he hath purposed in himself: That in the dispensation of the fulness of times he might gather together in one all things in Christ, both which are in Heaven, and which are on earth; even in him: In whom also we HAVE obtained an inheritance, being predestinated according to the purpose of him who worketh all things after the counsel of his own will: That we should be to the praise of his glory, who first trusted in Christ. In whom ye also trusted, after that ye heard the word of truth, the gospel of your salvation: in whom also after that ye believed, ye were sealed with that holy Spirit of promise, Which is the earnest of our inheritance until the redemption of the purchased possession, unto the praise of his glory."

Ephesians goes on to state in verses 18-23,
"The eyes of your understanding being enlightened; that ye may know what is the hope of his calling, and what the riches of the glory of his inheritance in the saints, And what is the exceeding greatness of his power to us-ward who believe, according to the working of his mighty power, Which he wrought in Christ, when he raised him from the dead, and set him at his own right hand in the heavenly places, Far above all principality, and power, and might, and dominion, and every name that is named, not only in this world, but also in that which is to come: And hath put all things under his feet,

117

and <u>gave him to be the head over all things to the church</u>, Which is his body, the fulness of him that filleth all in all."

In these scriptures, Paul reveals the intertwining of the eternal inheritance with the inheritance we have been given to operate in now. He shows that, through the life of Jesus, God has given us an inheritance in this present time and the time to come.

You have certain laws, rights, and an inheritance that you can enforce and partake of for your life RIGHT NOW! It's available to you because of who your Father is! He may have died before you were born, but you still have every right to His citizenship, His natural and legal rights, and the inheritance He has left for you to enjoy NOW!

I am so passionate about this because, as I told you earlier, my natural dad didn't leave me anything. My whole inheritance was confined to a light blue suitcase.

He did leave some demons that I have had to conquer and take ground back from. He left some governing laws that ruled our family for many generations, rules that I have had to break in Jesus' name.

So, to know that my heavenly Father has left me an inheritance that I can enjoy makes me excited. I refuse to give up the enjoyment to the fullest of the life my Father has given me to. I will receive everything He has purposed for me to have, and I will leave a greater inheritance for my children. This is the marking of a great man or woman.

Jesus even told us in John 14:12, "*Verily, verily, I say unto you, He that believeth on me, the works that I do shall he do also; and greater works than these shall he do; because I go unto my Father.*"

His desire for His children is that we do GREATER WORKS, accomplish greater things, defeat more devils, conquer more land, heal more of the sick, establish more for His kingdom, and perform more miracles!

This is what I want for you to do after reading this book. Take the reins of your life and go be great!

Jesus has paid the price, and He has given you the ability and the right to take the spoils. Go get everything that belongs to you!

Chapter 6

"All That I Have Is Yours"

It would be presumptuous to end this book and leave you thinking you know the rest of the story Jesus told in Luke 15.

We have talked about the father in the story. We have discussed the younger son in the story. However, there is one other character Jesus tells us about in the parable.

The Bible says in Luke 15:25-32, "*Meanwhile the older son was in the field, and as he approached the house, he heard music and dancing. So he called one of the servants and asked what was going on. 'Your brother has returned,' he said, 'and your father has killed the fattened calf, because he has him back safe and sound. The older son became angry and refused to go in. So his father came out and pleaded with him. But he answered his father, 'Look, all these years I have served you and never disobeyed a commandment of yours. Yet you never gave me even a young goat so I could celebrate with my friends. But when this son of yours returns from squandering your wealth with prostitutes, you kill the fattened calf for him!' Son, you are always with me,' the father said, 'and all that is mine is yours. But it was fitting to celebrate and be glad, because this brother of yours was dead and is alive again; he was lost and is found.*"

As the younger of the two sons demanded his inheritance, and then left, only to spend everything he was given on riotous living, the older son stayed home. The elder son stayed committed to his father. He stayed committed to his work and to his family. Upon hearing the celebration going on at the house while he was at work in the field, the elder son inquired about the celebration. The servants told the son that the father had called a celebration because his brother had come home. The elder son got very angry once he heard the father was celebrating the return of the younger son. He got so mad that he refused to partake in the celebration. The father then came out and met his son to address his actions.

I know that is a very quick overview, and there is so much that could be extracted from this portion of the story, but I want you to look at one statement that I feel reveals the heart of the Prodigal Father.

Once the father in the story confronts the elder son, who was angry about the celebration of his brother's return home, the elder brother expresses to his father why he was upset. He told his father that, while his brother was out wasting his father's wealth on prostitutes and sinful living, he continually served the father and never disobeyed him. He reminded his father that he never broke his trust.

This son's anger came from the confusion of not knowing why the father was celebrating his wayward son, when he never celebrated his faithful son. This is a legitimate question. How would the father respond to the elder son's concern?

The statement the father made to the elder son was this. "Son, you are always with me, and all that is mine is yours."

This statement not only shows the father's heart towards this son, but Jesus reveals to us the Father's heart towards His children.

He said first, *"you are with me always…"* He was saying he had no fear of his son's well being, because he knew where his son was and his condition of life. The father had this assurance because his son was with him. The father didn't have to be concerned for this son because he trusted in his father's ability to provide for him.

We can trust in our Father's ability to provide for us! He will always make a way for us to succeed in life!

I will never forget the first time my son, and later my daughter, drove out of my driveway without me. I was excited for them. I knew they could not wait to drive their car alone. But at the same time, I was very anxious because I was no longer in control of the vehicle that was transporting my babies. I never thought much about them being in the car with me. I knew their safety was found in my abilities and not their own. My fear, however, was immediate the moment they left my oversight.

 I believe this is why God has created spiritual parameters for us to live within. This is why He gave Adam and Eve certain parameters to live within while existing in the garden. These parameters were not to restrict them, but rather to protect them.

The standards God has given us to live by are not to restrict us or to keep us from having fun, but they are there to protect us.

God knows that, if we will live within those boundaries, He can protect us and control the "vehicle" that transports us through life. It's when we choose to live outside of God's divine will, or in other words, outside His parameters, that we are left to our own abilities and provision. However, when we choose to stay in our Father's presence and within His Kingdom principles, everything we need is supplied.

The second part of the father's statement to his elder son brings us another revelation of God's heart for His children.

The man told his son, "*all that I have is yours.*" This is the heart of the Prodigal Father. Everything that the Father has is, without question, available to His children. This is not a prosperity gospel; it is a Kingdom principle!

It is the heart of the Father for us, that every need we have He has already supplied. The Bible says in Psalms 84:11 "*For the LORD God is a sun and shield; The LORD gives grace and glory; No good thing does He withhold from those who walk uprightly.*"

A Prodigal Father withholds no good thing from His children. Everything He has belongs to His children.

Again, Philippians 4:19 states, "*And my God will supply all your needs according to His riches in glory in Christ Jesus.*"

Paul is telling God's children in Philippi the same thing the father in the parable told his son. He was saying, "I didn't throw a party for you and give you special gifts because everything I have is already yours!"

My daddy had a truck that I loved so much. I mentioned it in an earlier chapter. Not just anyone could jump in Daddy's truck and take it for a drive, but I could.

I would wash that truck, clean the inside, and take off down the road. All my buddies wanted to drive it, but they were not allowed. Why couldn't they drive Daddy's truck? Because they didn't have permission to drive it. They were friends, but they were not a son. I had access to the vehicle because it belonged to my daddy!

Daddy told me one time, "Son, you are welcome to drive my truck anytime you want to." He never had to tell me again. When I needed to go somewhere I jumped in Daddy's truck and took off down the road. Daddy didn't have to remind me every day that he gave me permission to drive his truck. I knew that I had access to it, because it belonged to my father.

May dad was a collector of hats. Back in the day, people had racks that they put hats on. They were called hat trees. They were stands about five feet tall, and at the top were arms that had hooks on which to hang your hats. These large hat racks were built to hold around ten to fifteen hats, which would be an extreme number of hats to own. But not for Daddy.

He had two of the largest hat racks made. He had so many hats that both hat racks had three or four hats hanging on each hook, and then a dozen or so hats were stacked on top. My daddy loved his hats.

He had all types of hats: baseball caps, double-billed hats, memorial hats, oversized hats, hats for the summer, hats for the winter, hats of all colors, shapes, and sizes. He even had a cowboy hat or two.

My dad loved to wear a hat. And because I wanted to be just like Daddy, I grew up wearing hats, as well. Just about every picture of me when I was a child shows me wearing a hat. Every day when I woke up at Daddy's house, I would walk over to those hat racks and choose a hat to wear. I didn't wake Daddy up and ask him if I could wear one. I didn't fill out a request form. I just grabbed a hat and went outside to play. I had a right to those hats because they belonged to my daddy. I had complete access to Daddy's hats because I was his son.

I know trucks and baseball caps may be things with little to no meaning to you, but don't miss the truth involved. I had access to certain things I needed, wanted, and desired in life simply because they belonged to my father. This was what the man in the story was explaining to his son.

This is the truth that God wants us to know. All that God has is ours!

Why? Because He is our Father!

As you prepare to close this book, possibly to never open it again, please don't close it without knowing this: You have a Father that owns everything. He is in charge of everything. He oversees everything. By that reason you have access to everything you need, desire, and want.

He will withhold no good thing from His children. He is the ultimate Prodigal Father. If you will love Him, trust Him, and seek Him with all your heart, He will fulfill every longing within your heart! He recklessly loves you! He is extravagant in displaying His heart toward you!

He wants to pour out Himself on you to the point it seems wasteful!

These are the words that define the word, "prodigal."

It means, to be reckless, extravagant, wasteful, and lavishing. These words describe how the Father reacts toward you. He is fulfilling. He is more than enough. He loves you with an everlasting love.

I wrote this book not to impress you with my literary skills, because I have none.

I did not try to dazzle you with wells of revelation. That's not what this book is about.

The motivation of my heart to pen the words that fill this book is simple. I wrote it for every young person who is searching for purpose with no voice of direction…

…for every young man who reaches for father-like arms to embrace him and, yet, finds none.

…for every young lady who has never felt the embrace of a man with no other motives than to express care for her.

…for every lady who has never heard a masculine voice identify her, choose her, and validate her.

…for every man that has crawled into a cave of isolation and loneliness because he never heard someone tell him that he was good enough and met all expectations.

I want you to know the heart of God is to fill you with purpose. He wants to be the arms that embrace you and never let you go again. He desires to be the everlasting embrace that brings you identification, validation, and purpose.

God longs to lead you out of the caves of isolation and loneliness by revealing to you your true self worth. He will communicate to you how important you are to Him and to the Kingdom of God. All you have to do is love Him, trust Him, and put Him first in every moment.

I pray that your faith has been strengthened. I trust that your heart has been softened. And I pray your life has been impacted.

Chase Jesus every day of your life, and always remember: The Prodigal Father is watching for you.

He can see you coming a great way off!

###

About the Author

David Edmondson, Jr., is Senior Pastor of Covenant Connections Church, Flowery Branch, Georgia.

He and his wife, Stephanie, have a son and a daughter, Noah and Reagan.

Additional copies of this book, as well as his other books, may be ordered online at covenantconnectionschurch.com

Find titles by the author also at www.amazon.com.

Other Books by David Edmondson include:

The Forming Process

The Joshua Generation

Coming Soon: The Man in the Office Next Door

Made in the USA
Columbia, SC
18 August 2019